Dartmouth Alumni Lectureships
on the Guernsey Center Moore Foundation

Season of 1922

CROSS CURRENTS
IN EUROPE TO-DAY

CROSS CURRENTS
IN EUROPE TO-DAY

BY

CHARLES A. BEARD, Ph.D., LL.D.

BOSTON

MARSHALL JONES COMPANY

PREFACE

The following pages form the substance of eight lectures on contemporary Europe delivered at Dartmouth College on the Guernsey Center Moore Foundation in June, 1922. The lectures were in fact informal and in the delivery many passages in the manuscript were materially reduced. The reader may be assured that the discourses were not as formidable as the printed pages might imply, and the auditors who did me the honor of attending the lectures may here discover that some of the most casual remarks were based upon independent inquiry. The volume is not a thesis, but a collection of notes pertinent, I hope, to the great case of Mankind *vs.* Chaos.

Charles A. Beard

New Milford, Conn.

CONTENTS

LECTURE   PAGE

PREFACE   V

I. DIPLOMATIC REVELATIONS: FRANCO-RUS-
SIAN   I

II. DIPLOMATIC REVELATIONS: ENGLISH UNDER-
STANDINGS   28

III. DIPLOMATIC REVELATIONS: THE CENTRAL
POWERS   56

IV. THE ECONOMIC OUTCOME OF THE WAR . .   83

V. THE NEW CONSTITUTIONS OF EUROPE . .   140

VI. THE RUSSIAN REVOLUTION   163

VII. THE RISE OF NEW PEASANT DEMOCRACIES .   182

VIII. SOCIALISM AND THE LABOR MOVEMENT .   202

IX. AMERICA AND THE BALANCE OF POWER . .   239

CONCLUSIONS   263

NOTE ON SOURCES FOR I. II. AND III. . .   273

BIBLIOGRAPHY   276

CROSS CURRENTS
IN EUROPE TO-DAY

CROSS CURRENTS IN EUROPE TO-DAY

I

DIPLOMATIC REVELATIONS: FRANCO-RUSSIAN

THE study of European affairs is no academic exercise for Americans; it runs to the roots of our national destiny. Our fate is not fashioned by domestic policies alone. Indeed, no wise domestic policies can be framed without reference to the course of world events. There has been no general war in Europe for more than two hundred years in which America has not taken part. As English colonies we participated in the War of the Spanish Succession at the opening of the eighteenth century; as an independent nation we shared in the responsibilities of the World War at the beginning of the twentieth century. Every concept of civic duty in war and peace, every dream of national grandeur has rested and must rest at bottom upon some foundation of international policy.

True as this was in 1914, it is still more true today. In foreign trade, in mercantile marine, in world finance, in sea power—in all matters respecting responsibilities and menaces in the international sphere—the United States has marched in seven league boots since August 1, 1914. Rome in the days of the first Triumvirate, Britain under the administration of William Pitt, America at the hour of Lincoln's first inauguration faced no problems greater than those which confront the government and people of the United States today. Their own fate they might control, but it is not in their hands alone. A single shot at Serajevo may send boys from the hills of New England and the plains of Kansas to die upon the banks of the Piave. There is now a web of international relations—trade, finance, and intercourse—so fine in mesh and so tough in fibre that no sword can cut it. The East and the West have met and they are one. The world is an economic unit and the United States is being woven into the very fabric of that unity. To study the nature of the fabric and the operations that weave it—surely there is no greater obligation, public or private, than this.

In this spirit the topics which follow were chosen. These pages attempt no mere chronicle of a few momentous years. They do not deal with personalities as such. They pass no judgments upon the motives and policies of the actors in the great drama that opened on August 1, 1914. It is no part of my design to discuss the remote or immediate causes of the war or to consider in any form the question of responsibility for bringing that calamity upon mankind. These pages simply deal with facts and themes which, in my opinion, most vitally concern

Americans here and now confronted with the task of arriving at some worthy concept of national policy, domestic and foreign.

The task of selecting the material is necessarily a delicate one. Each of us must perforce see what is behind his own eyes. No person, aware of the mysteries and presences that surround the path of mankind, as it stumbles forward through the years, will have overweening confidence in his ability to divine the future through the murky shadows of the past. Still we cannot escape an obligation by confessing its difficulties and it may be that in a multitude of councils there is some wisdom along with much error.

From what has just been said, it is clear that no apology need be offered for devoting two lectures to the diplomatic methods of Europe which have recently been revealed to us by one of the strangest strokes of fortune in all history. Diplomacy, as a score of writers have warned us, is the danger point of democracy. The management of relations among nations must of necessity be entrusted to a small number of persons. No congress of 435 members, no parliament of 570 members could possibly carry on the diplomatic intercourse required by modern international life. How European diplomats have operated within their sphere during the past few years becomes therefore a theme of absorbing interest to Americans, for the gentlemen who sit around the council tables of Europe help to determine our fate as well as their own.

For many long years we have lived in the mists

of official propaganda. Shortly after the Great
War opened, each of the belligerent governments
published a volume of carefully selected papers.
The purpose in every case was the same, namely, to
prove the guilt of the enemy and the innocence of the
publisher. On the basis of these official papers, skillfully chosen by the parties to the case, editors, professors, and publicists wrote books, pamphlets, and
leading articles, all designed to support the official
theses put forward by their respective governments
and to stir up the war fever necessary to sustain
the fighting to the bitter end. The propriety of this
is not here questioned. In time of war reason as
well as law must be silent; but to continue fostering
in time of peace the passions of war surely has no
defenders among those who seek guidance for the
future in the experience of the past.

Had the war ended in a stalemate, our knowledge
of the origins of the conflict and the diplomatic
methods which precipitated it would be limited to
the official statements made by the gentlemen responsible for it. But the war did not end in a stalemate.
The several belligerents did not emerge with their
political machines intact. The Germans, during
their occupation of Belgium, searched the Belgian
archives and published sheaves of important secret
papers. The Bolsheviki, on overthrowing the old
Russian government, exposed to the gaze of the
astonished world the Secret Treaties and hundreds
of diplomatic documents relative to Entente diplomacy before the war. The German Social Democrats, after the November revolution, opened the

archives of Wilhelmstrasse. In Vienna, the downfall of the Dual Monarchy was followed by the publication of important papers taken from the Austrian foreign office. The archives of London, Paris, and Rome are still secure under lock and key, but the thousands of secret papers from other capitals enable us to form some idea of the marvels concealed from our gaze in those quarters.

Never before has a generation called upon to wage a great war been given an opportunity to discover the methods which precipitated the crisis from which it suffered. Usually fifty or a hundred years are allowed to pass before the public is given access to the pertinent papers; that is to say, when it is too late for citizens to form any judgment on current policies and practices, governments open their archives. But the fortunes of the last war proved an exception to the rule. Now within eight years of the opening of the conflict we have the most priceless records, the most secret documents, the most confidential memoranda revealing the spirit and technique of the diplomacy which preceded the war. We are now able to compare official theses with official facts and to measure propaganda against reality. The debts, deficits, indemnities, paper money, and industrial crisis from which Europe suffers present nothing new to students of human affairs, but the revelation of the methods which diplomats employed for years before the war is new and marvellous beyond anything that has happened since November 11, 1918.

Students of history and diplomacy knew, of course,

long before the Great War burst upon the world in
1914 that the embattled powers on both sides were
united by ties of some kind; but the nature of these
agreements, the extent of the obligations created, the
inner designs of the diplomatic negotiations accompanying them were all mysteries . In vain did members of parliamentary bodies elected by millions of
voters ask foreign ministers for explanations, details, and precise information. In vain did citizens,
editors, publicists, and political leaders demand to
know the character of the obligations which in the
hour of crisis the masses would be called upon to
assume. Their pleas and their demands alike met
indifference, contempt, or evasion. Behind closed
doors diplomats exchanged pledges and created situations which drove Europe relentlessly into the
abyss. Out of the millions that went forth to die,
out of the millions that stayed at home to suffer
and bear burdens, only a handful—a score or more—
knew by what process the terrible dénouement had
been brought to pass.

The remedy for this state of affairs in diplomacy
lies in no mere institutional changes. It lies in an
ever growing body of enlightened citizens who do
their own thinking and are not deceived by official
propaganda. They will find in the diplomatic revelations of the past five years lessons of prime importance for the future. Europe may live forever, if it
so chooses, under the shadow of diplomatic delusion
and deception, but it is not necessary, certainly it is
not expedient, that America should do so.

NEW MATERIALS ON RUSSIA'S BALKAN POLICY

We shall start with the Russian documents, for in the order of time, Russia was the first to bare her records. It is important however to warn the reader against forming any final conclusion until the data of the Austrian and German papers are all in. Even then it must be remembered that we are not dealing with the fundamental and underlying causes of the war, but with secret diplomacy as such.

Immediately after the overthrow of the Tsar in March, 1917, all kinds of rumors and reports about domestic dissensions over foreign policy began to flow out of Russia. The new revolutionary government, hard beset by a still more revolutionary peace party, found it difficult to defend the war program of the old régime and the avowed aims of the Allies. Indeed the revolutionary leaders in the streets, who were in time to possess the machinery of state, demanded a repudiation of all designs savoring of annexations, indemnities, and imperialism. When the Bolsheviki finally got possession of the government, they found it in keeping with their principles and useful in their tactics to discredit the policies of the Tsar. Accordingly they began to publish treaties, notes, and papers taken from the Russian archives all tending to show the imperialist ambitions of England, France, Italy, and the Tsar's government. In November, 1917, they gave out to the world a long report composed of notes and extracts from letters exchanged among the Entente Allies relative to the proposed distribution of the spoils at the close of the war—the famous "Secret Treaties." Among other things, England was to take a benevolent attitude toward Russian pretensions at the Straits and receive in return adequate compensations. Russia was to have a free hand in arranging her Polish frontiers; France was to have Alsace-Lorraine and create a neutral autonomous state on the left bank of the Rhine. In the months and years that followed, the Bolsheviki continued to issue selections from the Russian archives. Some of these were published in booklets and others in the official newspapers, *Pravda* and *Isvestia*.

In these documents we may trace, as under the rays of a great searchlight, the important relations of Russia to Europe and Asia from 1908 onward. In particular, is it easy to trace the plans adopted by Russia to counteract the relentless economic advance of Germany and Austria in southeastern Europe.

The story opens with the record of measures to be taken in the Balkans. In January, 1908, after its accounts had been settled with England and Japan the Russian government had a free hand and began a forward policy in southeastern Europe. This policy, in its general terms, had been agreed upon several months before the annexation of Bosnia and Herzegovina by Austria. It was discussed at a grand council of the civil and military authorities held early in the year; but it was not immediately put into active force. There was no want of desire but, as the military men pointed out, the Russian army had not recovered from the defeat at the hands of Japan and the Tsar, who had just escaped from a revolution by the skin of his teeth, did not dare to risk another crisis soon. So for several months, the Russian foreign office was circumspect though determined. It confined its activities to very moderate and restrained diplomatic maneuvers preparatory to something more vigorous to follow.

When later in the year, Austria-Hungary seized Bosnia and Herzegovina, the Serbs appealed to St. Petersburg for aid; but the Russian government, aware that it was in no condition for another war, gave counsels of caution while adding assurances of something substantial to come later. In October, 1908, the Russian ambassador, Isvolski, said to the Serbian minister at Paris: "Serbia will lose nothing as a result of the step taken by Austria, but will actually gain from it. You Serbs cannot think of dislodging Austria-Hungary from Bosnia and Herzegovina by arms. . . . Hitherto we have always sustained Serbia and we shall support her in the future, always and with all possible means." A few months later, namely in March, 1909, the Russian government informed Serbia that "when her equipment is ready, Russia will renew the matter with Austria-Hungary. Serbia should not go to war, because that would be suicide. . . . Conceal your intentions and prepare yourselves because the days of joy will come."

From that time forward, as the records clearly

show, Russian diplomacy, restless, aggressive, and covert, was directed toward one end: the formation of combinations of power and the pursuit of measures likely to dissolve the Austro-Hungarian empire in a general European war. This is the substance of the first revelations from the Russian archives. Russian diplomats, having made sure of Asiatic matters by understandings with England and Japan, had firmly resolved, by 1908, to break up the Dual Monarchy. For six years they bent every energy to that enterprise. The Tsar's agents knew that Germany was allied with Austria and would not stand idly by while Russia and Serbia carried out their plans. For that reason Russia resolved to make the issue general, drawing into the affair both France and England. Meanwhile Russia kept Serbian nationalism aflame by assuring the Serbs that the day of liberation would come. In January, 1914, the Serbian minister, Pashitch, asked the Tsar whether he would give one of the grand duchesses in marriage to the Serbian Crown Prince. The Tsar was delighted with the idea, although he declined to dictate in an affair of the heart. Then the minister, in a burst of ecstacy, said: "She would enjoy the affection of all the Serbian people, and if God and circumstances permit she will become the queen of all the Slav nations of the South. Her glory and her influence will spread throughout the Balkan peninsula." Such was the grand Serb dream: Break up Austria-Hungary, unite the South Slavs, and bind Russia and Slavia in matrimony. So

Serbia and Russia set out together on their way to the "joyous days."

On the lengths to which the Russian leaders were prepared to go and the means which they were willing to employ, there are two important letters from the Russian archives. In 1911, the Russian ambassador at Paris wrote home: "If we have decided to raise the question of the Straits [the Turkish question], it is of the highest importance in that regard to have a favourable press here. Unfortunately, I am in that respect deprived of the most important means, since my insistent requests for funds for the press have produced no results. I shall naturally do all that is in my power, but it is a matter in which public opinion, for traditional reasons, is against us. As an example of the utility of having money for the press, I may cite the affair of Tripoli. I know how Tittoni (Italian ambassador at Paris) won over the leading French journals *avec la main largement ouverte.*"

This compelling argument evidently had the desired result at St. Petersburg, for shortly afterward, M. Isvolski wrote to his superior at home: "I am trying to maintain the desirable feeling in governmental and political circles and at the same time am attempting to influence the press. In this respect very remarkable results have been attained, thanks partly to measures previously taken. As you know I do not distribute the subsidies directly, but the distribution is made in co-operation with the French minister, and has already had the necessary effect.

I myself am endeavoring to guide the more important newspapers in Paris, such as the 'Temps,' the 'Journal des Debats,' and the 'Echo' through personal influence."

THE FRANCO-RUSSIAN ALLIANCE

It was obvious to the directors of the Muscovite foreign policy that Russia alone could not effect a dissolution of Austria-Hungary and bring about a realization of the grand Pan-Slav, Pan-Serb dream. It was well known that Germany and Austria Hungary, to say nothing of Italy, were knit together in a firm alliance and that the former would not stand idly by while her only undoubted friend in Europe was overwhelmed in battle. It was necessary, therefore, to secure active assistance from France and if possible from England. This was an accepted axiom in Russian diplomatic circles. The formula is set forth with great clearness in a letter from the Russian ambassador at London directed to his home government on November 20, 1912. After speaking of a conversation with Sir Edward Grey, who disclaimed any intentions of aggression against Germany, the ambassador said: "He has told me enough to prove to us that under certain special conditions, England would enter the war. For this, in my opinion, two conditions are necessary: in the first place, the active intervention of France must make this war a general one; secondly it is absolutely necessary that the responsibility for the aggression fall upon our opponents. I believe it is imperative that we keep this point well in mind. First of all it involves the necessity of maintaining the principle of our own disinterestedness. . . . It will be necessary to emphasize the aggressive character of Austrian and German policy. . . . The question of who is to be the aggressor will be of greatest significance. Only under these circumstances would the British government have the support of public opinion which the government needs for energetic action. Grey and his ministerial colleagues are, no doubt, occupied with reflections of this kind. I see the echo of them in the answer he has given to the question I put to him." Without doubt, this Russian analysis of the problem in 1912 was a sound one. If the design was to succeed, it was imperative that the active intervention of France should make the war a general one, in which England might participate, under special conditions, particularly if the burden of aggression fell upon the Teutonic powers.

The Russian approach to France was natural and easy. The two countries had been united by a firm alliance since 1891, and their diplomatic negotiations were close and active. The exact nature of the alliance, however, was not known outside the official circles. Again and again questions had been put by curious members of the French Parliament, but the ministry had carefully avoided giving any precise information.

It was not until after the Bolsheviki had begun to publish the old Russian archives that the French government thought it wise and fitting to let the public know the exact nature of the obligations that bound France and Russia under the agreement of

1891. In 1918 the French ministry issued its famous Yellow Book containing a number of selected papers bearing on the alliance. These have been subjected to many critical examinations. A member of the Institute, M. Welschinger, for example, has reprinted most of the papers and illuminated them by invaluable comment in his *L'Alliance Franco-Russe*. In this small but valuable treatise we can trace the history of this fateful combination of powers.

Without going back of 1886, it appears that Katkof, the editor of the *Moscow Gazette,* and Elie de Cyon began in that year their propaganda for a Franco-Russian understanding. We may dismiss as hardly relevant the German accusation that Katkof received money from de Lesseps to carry on his operations. The next year, between May and December, important relations were established between the Russian Ministry of Finance and the Haute-Banque Française which ended in an arrangement with the Rothschilds for a grand debt conversion and opened the French financial market wide for Russian loans.

Between 1880 and 1905, according to Welschinger's estimates, at least sixteen Russian loans were floated in France amounting all together to about twelve billion francs, not counting underwritings for many railways, banking institutions, and private enterprises. After 1905 the amount was increased by still greater advances. "The success of the Russian loan of 1888," remarks Welschinger, "facilitated by the Crédit Foncier, had a remarkable effect upon the concord so heartily desired."

Newspaper propaganda was under way. Financial relations were being forged in bonds of gold. The French government sent a squadron to the Baltic on a pleasure trip, and the Tsar received it with a great show of affection even though it involved his standing hat in hand while the Marseillaise, played by a band of sansculottes, beat upon his imperial ears! At the same time, General Boisdeffre, of the French general staff, attended the grand Russian manoeuvres and was delightfully entertained by his new companions-in-arms. The Marquis de Breteuil, a French gentleman of the old school, visited the Russian ambassador at a watering place and discussed with him, quite informally of course, the idea of an entente between the two countries. Then the head of the Russian foreign office wrote, in a general way, that a cordial understanding between the two countries would be the best guarantee of peace and necessary to maintain a just balance of European powers. The French foreign minister replied favorably, saying that he was prepared to "examine the suggestions" on the subject of an alliance as a protection in case of a threat of hostilities on the part of the Triple Alliance.

After many pourparlers and much correspondence, the understanding was embodied in an exchange of notes, formally concluded on August 21, 1891. The text of the document is very short. The object of the accord is said to be the maintenance of the general peace. The two governments agree to act in concert on every question that threatens to put peace in jeopardy. They also agree to discuss at once the measures necessary for simultaneous coöperation in case of war.[1]

The gentlemen's understanding was supplemented by conversations between representatives of the two general staffs—conversations which bore fruit in a military convention formally concluded on January 4, 1894. This convention provided for combined and instant operations in case either of the parties was attacked by any of the powers of the Triple Alliance, for immediate mobilization without preliminary notice, and for forward movements to the frontiers. The number of men to be employed against Germany was agreed upon, future conferences were provided for, a no-separate-peace clause was inserted, the duration of the convention was fixed at the life of the Triple Alliance, and strict secrecy was pledged.

Fêtes, exchanges of visits, military conferences, felicitations, and vague allusions to the new friendship between France and Russia followed the ratification of the agreements. There was an abundance of conversations and correspondence. But no one out-

---

[1] This remained a secret until 1918. As late as 1916, a professional student of European diplomacy, Professor Hayes, had to write of this alliance: "Of the exact steps by which the friendship of the two nations was transformed into a defensive alliance between the two governments little is actually known, but it appears that a diplomatic protocol for an alliance was signed in 1891 and that a military convention was agreed upon in 1894." If this is what a careful scholar could find out about the alliance, what must the average French or Russian soldier have known about it?

side of the official circles knew just what had taken place. Wise men exchanged knowing looks and did all that they could to strengthen the ties thus formed. The French purse was opened wide to Russian borrowers. The Paris police were more active in apprehending Russian refugees from justice. Criticism of the Russian autocracy was outlawed in polite circles.

As time went on it occurred to French diplomats that the accord was not exactly in the precise terms which the situation demanded. In the summer of 1899 M. Delcassé broached the subject in a conversation with the Tsar. He pointed out two very significant things: First, that the accord was a purely defensive one, directed against the Triple Alliance and designed merely to maintain the peace of Europe, and secondly, that the military convention would come to an end with a dissolution of the Triple Alliance. The interesting suggestions profoundly impressed the Tsar, especially as M. Delcassé accompanied them by these ingenious reflections: "What would happen if the Triple Alliance should be dissolved otherwise than by the will of its members; if, for example, the Emperor Francis Joseph, who appears at the moment to be the sole bond of union between the rival, yes, belligerent, races of Austria-Hungary, should suddenly die; if Austria were menaced by a dislocation which perhaps is desired in some quarters, which perhaps one might favor, and in which one, in any case, might be led to wish to take part? What matter is more likely to break the general peace and destroy the

European balance of power? And what matter
more seriously requires the union of France and
Russia not only in the same design but in its execution? Now it is exactly at the precise hour when
the military convention should come into play that
it ceases to exist; born of the Triple Alliance it would
vanish with it."

The argument of M. Delcassé, the implications of
which are too patent to call for comment, touched the
Tsar in a tender spot. An exchange of notes was
at once begun ending in a revision of the accord of
1891. The original understanding stated that
France and Russia were desirous of maintaining the
general peace; the revision of 1899 adds "and the
equilibrium of the European powers." The original military compact provided that it should last
as long as the Triple Alliance; the revision of 1899
stipulates that it shall remain in force as long as the
diplomatic agreement concluded for the purpose of
safeguarding the common and permanent interests of
the two countries.

From year to year the military bonds of the high
contracting parties were strengthened by numerous
conversations. Finally, in 1912, the Tsar expressed
to the French ambassador his desire for a naval convention drawn along the lines of the military understanding. The appropriate negotiations were held
and in midsummer the new document was signed.
This agreement provided for naval co-operation in
case of war. The details were to be worked out
by supplementary conversations. The proper
naval authorities were instructed to study the vari-

ous hypotheses of war, to correspond directly, to arrange strategic programs, and to keep their affairs under the bond of secrecy.

In the light of what we now know of the Russo-French alliance, of the modifications made in the text in 1899, and of the long military negotiations, between the two powers, the debates that arose in the French Parliament from time to time between 1891 and 1914 on the fateful agreement take on a new significance. More than once, members of the Chamber of Deputies attempted to draw the ministers out on the question of the exact relations established by the understanding. In November, 1896, M. Millerand asked whether it was a simple treaty or a military convention that bound the two countries and what were the extent and bearing of the agreement. In the midst of considerable disturbance he expressed astonishment that he, a deputy, was not permitted to inquire about the nature of the accord. "Is the republic," he exclaimed, "the government of the people bound to hand over to a few men the uncontested direction of its destiny?" M. Jaurès said that it followed from the uniform silence of the minister on the subject that the treaty was an illusion or more likely that the government of France had lost the right to speak freely to France. The minister of foreign affairs replied simply that the country and all reasonable statesmen approved the Russian policy. He added that everything that could and should be safely said in public had already been said. He refused to go into details and the Chamber approved his reticence.

Two years later another debate arose. Again M. Millerand and M. Jaurès wanted to know the exact nature of the treaty. Once more the minister of foreign affairs replied simply in generalities. He told them that it was impossible to make known the terms of the entente—the facts spoke so loudly that it was not necessary to say anything more. For the Chamber of Deputies that laconic remark was sufficient to warrant a vote of approval.

Thirteen years more elapsed. Momentous events had taken place. All members of the inner circle knew that Europe trembled on the verge of a crisis. On April 6, 1911, a stormy debate arose in the Senate. Pacifists assailed the treaty as a cause of war. Intransigents wanted to know whether the treaty had not merely guaranteed the status quo to the advantage of Germany. That was a delicate subject, but the minister of foreign affairs did not shrink from it. He replied hotly that the treaty did not merely guarantee the status quo but covered all eventualities and permitted the contracting parties to conceal their policies and draw all possible advantages from the concert. He warned them that the matter of Alsace-Lorraine would have to be settled before the pacifist idea of general arbitration could be adopted—a statement which brought the assembly to its feet. "We are pacific," he declared, "but we say that too often and sometimes too loudly." He closed by telling them that France would be firm in respecting all rights and equally firm in discharging all her duties. Once more the answer of the minister proved satis-

factory to the great majority of his colleagues.   The
grand alliance remained curtained in darkness.

Running through the serried documents is the
thread of the lost provinces.   The Tsar once remarked to M. de Montebello: "I often hear
people speak of the ideas of revanche which exist
among you and are used as a menace.   I see no justi-
fication for that.   You would not be good Frenchmen if you did not cherish the thought that a day
will come in which you may enter into possession
of your lost provinces; but between that sentiment
and the idea of a provocation to realize it there
is a great distance, and you have proved it many
times—and have proved it again—that you wish
peace above all and that you know how to wait with
dignity."   While the negotiations were on between
the military men of the two countries, the Russian
representative frankly asked this question: "When
you once have your military convention signed will
you not precipitate things and make war?"   It was
for that very reason that the Tsar once insisted on
a provision declaring the treaty void if war was
provoked by France; but his fears seem to have been
allayed—to some extent, as the above remark implied.

In the course of the debates in the French Parliament, the same theme came up in various forms.
In 1896, M. Millerand wanted to know what advantages had been secured in return for the engage-
ments with Russia and whether obligations of active friendship had been imposed on the new ally.
He bluntly asked whether it was necessary for

France to resign herself to the acceptance of the
fait accompli—making an evident allusion to Alsace-
Lorraine that called forth great applause.   He was
especially eager to know whether the country incurred the risk of being abandoned in an hour of
grave danger.   In the later debates, the same burning issue arose and the minister for foreign affairs,
while refusing to be precise, gave his auditors to
understand that the accord with Russia did not pro-
vide for a mere guarantee of the status quo, but
for all eventualities.   It was not necessary to say
more.

FRANCO-RUSSIAN DIPLOMATIC NEGOTIATIONS, 1912-1914

Such was the union between France and Russia
when the latter decided, in 1908, upon a liquidation of the Austro-Hungarian empire; but for the
moment the outlook at Paris was not favorable.
It was not until 1912 that the Russian diplomats
at work on the new forward policy found conditions in France somewhat in line with their purposes.
In that year there came a turn in French affairs.
The action of Germany in forcing a readjustment of
the Moroccan estate in 1911, aroused France and
was represented in the intransigent French press as
a piece of brutal aggression.   In January, 1912, the
Caillaux cabinet, committed to a policy of friendly
relations with Germany, was forced out of office,
and there then came to power M. Raymond Poincaré, an avowed champion of peace, "united with

firmness and preparedness." An eminent French publicist, M. Albin remarks of M. Poincaré: "From his clear and trained mind, from his firm will, from his character as a Lorrainer, little given to accommodations, France expected enlightened direction, a beneficent influence on political events, and in foreign affairs a firm and active policy worthy of the past of France, worthy of the rôle she had played in the world and of the place she should occupy in the future. . . . As the result of a coincidence due to no mere play of ministerial combinations, M. Poincaré, at the same time, took charge of the portfolio of foreign affairs." For a year M. Poincaré directed the French foreign policy as prime minister. Then he was elected President and for seven years more exerted a powerful influence on French foreign and domestic policies.

It is evident from the documents taken from the Russian archives and published to the world, that M. Poincaré took an active, rather than a passive, attitude in the matter of Russian relations. If the Russian ambassador at Paris had found negotiations difficult before 1912, he had no reason to complain upon the installation of M. Poincaré. Shortly after the latter became prime minister and minister of foreign affairs, M. Isvolski, the Tsar's representative in France, wrote home a very illuminating letter to the effect that the new French leader was taking the initiative and that Russia should by all means meet him half way. A part of this note follows: "M. Poincaré has several times asked me what I know about the exchange of opinions concerning Balkan affairs which, according to reports in the newspapers and those coming from other sources, had taken place between you and the Vienna cabinet; in connection with this, he reminded me once more of his readiness at almost any moment to enter into negotiations concerning these matters and gave me to understand that he expects us to give him the same thorough information concerning our negotiations with Vienna that he had received from the London cabinet after the journey of Lord Haldane to Berlin. I write all this to you in the fullest sincerity, for it seems to me that it is above all important to keep in mind and to meet half way the purposes which M. Poincaré expressed to me upon his entrance into office. The present prime minister and minister for foreign affairs is an exceedingly great personality and his cabinet shows itself as the strongest combination of power that has existed for a long period of years."

Later in the same year, M. Isvolski wrote home a very important letter. He had it from M. Poincaré that, in the event of a crisis in the Balkans, such as an attack by Austria on Serbia, Russia would receive "the most sincere and most energetic support" from France during the diplomatic stage of the negotiations. In this stage, M. Poincaré had said, the French ministry would not have the support of Parliament or of public opinion, but that was only the preliminary. M. Poincaré went on to add that if diplomatic negotiations led by Russia resulted in armed intervention on the part of Ger-

many, France "would not hesitate a minute in fulfilling her obligations towards Russia." This letter
which flashes light into the Balkan darkness must
be reproduced at length:

"M. Poincaré told me that the French government is first of all considering the question of possible international eventualities. It quite realizes
that this or that event, as for instance, the destruction of Bulgaria by Turkey or an attack upon Serbia
by Austria might force Russia to give up its passive
attitude and first take diplomatic steps, to be followed afterwards by military measures against Turkey or Austria. According to assurances received
by us from the French government we can in such a
case count upon the most sincere and most energetic
diplomatic support on the part of France. In this
phase of events, the government of the Republic
would not be in a position, however, to obtain the
sanction of Parliament or of public opinion for
any active military measures. If the conflict with
Austria, however, should result in an armed inter-
ference on the part of Germany, France would, as
a matter of course, look upon this as a 'casus foederis' and not hesitate a minute to fulfil its obligations towards Russia. 'France,' M. Poincaré
added, 'is undoubtedly peaceably inclined, neither
looking for war nor desiring it. If Germany goes
against Russia, however, this state of mind will
change immediately,' and he is convinced that in
this case Parliament, as well as public opinion will
unanimously back the government's resolution to
render armed assistance to Russia.

"M. Poincaré further told me that, in view of the critical position in the Balkans, the highest authorities of the French Military-Command are studying with increasing attention all possible military eventualities and it was known to him that expert and responsible personages held an extremely optimistic view of the Russo-French chances in case of a general collision. This optimistic view is based on the value attributed to the diversion exercised by the united forces of the Balkan states, in drawing off a corresponding number of Austro-Hungarian forces. The fact that Italy is deprived of freedom of movement, owing to the African war and a special agreement with France, is another point in favor of Russia and France.

"As to the position in the Mediterranean, the resolution just taken of removing the third French squadron from Brest to Toulon has enhanced the supremacy of the French fleet in these waters. This resolution, M. Poincaré added, has been taken in concurrence with England and forms the further development and completion of the agreements formerly concluded between the French and British naval staffs."

A few weeks later in the same year, the Russian ambassador at Paris wrote home again, this time in a more decisive tone, reporting a conversation with M. Poincaré. Here is the important part of the Communication: " 'It is for Russia,' he remarked to me, to take the initiative in a question [the Austro-Serbian affair] in which she is interested above all others; whilst it is France's task to give her full and active support. If the French government were to take the initiative itself, it would either run the risk of exceeding the intentions of its ally or of not doing them full justice. . . . All in all,' Poincaré added, 'this means that if Russia makes war France will also make war, because we know that Germany will stand by Austria in this question.' In answer to my inquiry whether he knew England's view in this matter, Poincaré said, that according to his information, the London cabinet would for the moment confine itself to promising Russia its entire diplomatic support, but that this would not under certain conditions exclude more energetic assistance."

It is no doubt hazardous to draw conclusions from these documents, but two or three seem to be unavoidable. Russia decided early in 1908 on an active policy which could not fail to lead to a clash with Austria. France later gave her a free hand either without knowing what the program of St. Petersburg really was or with full knowledge of the policy and the consequences. There is no doubt that the French prime minister told Russia to take the initiative and promised active diplomatic support. It is clear also that the French prime minister was aware that this might lead to a general war by drawing in Germany and involving France. It may be that circumstances warranted M. Poincaré in following this line, but one thing is certain: nobody in France outside of the diplomatic circle knew what commitments were being made—commitments fraught with such agony for mankind.

II

DIPLOMATIC REVELATIONS: ENGLISH UNDERSTANDINGS

STUDENTS of European politics who watched the drift of English foreign policy between 1898 and 1914 were well aware of certain marked tendencies. By an alliance with Japan consummated in 1902, by a treaty with France concluded in 1904, clearing up all points of controversy between the two countries, and by a treaty with Russia signed in 1907 settling disputed questions, England had removed a number of dangerous issues in foreign affairs. In defending the Japanese alliance against the advocates of isolation, Lord Lansdowne said in 1902: "What do we see on all sides? We observe a tendency to ever-increasing naval and military armaments involving ever-increasing burdens upon the people for the defence of whose countries these armaments are accumulated. There is also this—that in these days war breaks out with a suddenness which was unknown in former days when nations were not, as they are now, armed to the teeth and ready to enter upon hostilities at any moment. . . . If there be no countervailing objections, the country which has the good fortune to possess allies is more to be envied than the country which is without them." The renewal of the Japanese alli-

ance in another form in 1907 became doubly significant, because within a period of a few months the
world learned of the continuance of the Anglo-
Japanese arrangements and the formation of a
Franco-Japanese, a Russo-Japanese, and an Anglo-
Russian agreement. There were in addition, as
we now know, secret treaties and negotiations between Russia and Japan, with England's consent,
which had a vital relation to the alignment of military and naval powers for the Great War. But
English statesmen denied all allegations to the effect
that these arrangements were connected with a de-
liberate policy of "encircling" Germany. They
said at the time that all these agreements grew out
of the laudable desire of England to be at peace
with the world and clear away all possible sources
of misunderstandings with neighboring powers.

SIR EDWARD GREY OF THE ANGLO-FRENCH ENTENTE

It was known in 1914, however, that England's
understandings with France had gone beyond mere
cordiality, for the Moroccan crises of 1906 and
1911 had revealed a close coöperation of the two
powers in the dealings with Germany. Still the exact character of the relations between the two countries was shrouded in mystery. The naturally sus-
picious in England thought that some positive agreements as to coöperation in war had been secretly
made. There were rumors in the press to that
effect and more than once the matter came up for
discussion in Parliament. In March, 1913, for ex-

ample, a responsible statesman, Lord Hugh Cecil, put the question very bluntly to the government: "There is a very general belief that this country is under an obligation, not a treaty obligation, but an obligation arising owing to an assurance given by the Ministry in the course of diplomatic negotiations, to send a very large armed force out of this country to operate in Europe. This is the general belief." To this clear-cut query the Prime Minister, Mr. Asquith, made a categorical reply: "I ought to say that it is not true."

Twice during the next year the question was again raised as to (1) whether the country was free from all obligations to engage in military operations on the continent, and (2) whether there were any unpublished agreements with Russia or France which would "restrain or hamper" the freedom of the government or the Parliament in making a decision about taking part in a European war. On both occasions the answer of the responsible ministers was emphatically in the negative. The world was given the impression that there was no obligation on the part of England to come to the aid of France on the continent and that no understandings existed with either Russia or France which in any way bound, restricted, or hampered the government and Parliament of England in case a crisis arose in Europe.

When on August 3, 1914, the great decision had to be taken, Sir Edward Grey, in his memorable plea for the support of France, revealed for the first time the nature of the conversations and un-

derstandings that had been drawing the two countries together during the previous ten years.   He
explained how the French admiralty, on the basis
of its belief in English friendship and the arrangements made with the English admiralty, had concentrated its fleet in the Mediterranean and left
the Atlantic coast of France undefended and how
the day before he had assured France that, if the
German fleet came out, England would protect the
defenceless ports across the channel.   He explained
how naval conversations extending over many years
had prepared for the immediate and effective co-
operation of the two powers in case of war.   But,
he added, it had always been understood that these
consultations did not "restrict the freedom of either
government to decide at any future time whether or
not to assist the other by armed force."   What,
therefore, was the nature of the obligation?   On
this point, Sir Edward said: "How far that entails
an obligation, let every man look into his own heart
and his own feelings and construe the extent of the
obligation for himself.   I construe it myself as
I feel it, but I do not wish to urge upon anyone else
more than their feelings dictate as to what they
should feel about the obligation."

To say the least, this was a most extraordinary
statement.   Sir Edward Grey had been carrying on
secret negotiations and conversations with France
for many years.   Complete plans for the landing
of English troops on the continent had been made
and the disposal of the naval forces of the two
countries had been agreed upon.   In the presence

of a crisis Sir Edward had to reveal them for the first time to an astounded Parliament. He pointed out that in the written records of the negotiations and understandings, full freedom of action had been reserved. Nevertheless, some kind of an obligation existed. Its extent he left to the consciences of the gentlemen who just heard of it for the first time in their lives—gentlemen who in the crisis had but one choice left to them. As for himself, he felt that England now had obligations of friendship with France that compelled coöperation in war. Still, he did not "wish to urge upon any one else more than their feelings dictate as to what they should feel about the obligation." Whatever view one takes of this amazing revelation, one must admit that it makes strange reading beside the statement, made by the same speaker earlier in that very year, to the effect that "there were no unpublished agreements which would restrict or hamper the freedom of the government or of Parliament to decide whether or not Great Britain should participate in a war."

Judgments upon Sir Edward Grey's revelations have varied. A highly critical English writer, Mr. E. D. Morel, in attacking what he regards as the bitter fruit of secret diplomacy, summarizes his opinion of the "conversations" arranged secretly under Sir Edward's management as follows: "These particular 'conversations' meant the elaboration of an entire plan of campaign, replete in every detail, affecting the disembarkation and transport over rail and road of an expeditionary force of

165,000 men—or whatever the exact number may have been—with enormous quantities of cannon, horses, motors, waggons, stores, and all the impedimenta of a modern army. As with the military, so with the naval 'conversations.'

"You may speak of an understanding whereby France concentrated her fleet in the Mediterranean and left her western and northern coast line undefended, in order to leave us freer to concentrate in the North Sea as a 'conversation' of no binding force until authorized by Parliament. But this is the sort of conversation which decides the destinies of nations, and when carried on in secret leaves the nations concerned entirely helpless to control the outcome. The secret conversations begun in 1906 and thenceforth persisted in constituted morally speaking a pledge given to France by the most powerful personalities in the British Liberal ministry to join with France in the event of a war between France and her only potential foe, Germany. Materially speaking they constituted an Anglo-French military and naval alliance. I can understand the argument which says that it was right to give that pledge. I can even understand the argument which says that it was right, having given that pledge, to deny to the House of Commons that it had been given. But I do not understand the argument which says that the moral obligation and the material fact alike meant nothing, until at the eleventh hour the House of Commons became aware of both and endorsed them."

Another English writer, at the opposite pole of

opinion from Mr. Morel, namely, Lord Esher, in his book on Lord Kitchener, speaking of this curious "obligation" revealed by Sir Edward Grey on August 3, says: "To Mr. Asquith the nation owes the redemption of its honor, for although he repudiated the assumption of a definite agreement with France, he has been credited by the French ambassador, M. Cambon, with the fixed determination of fulfilling the moral obligation to that country to come to her assistance in case of an unprovoked attack when the occasion arose; for the obligation, as Mr. Asquith knew well, was the inevitable sequel to the conversations which had been carried on between the General Staffs of the two Armies for some years. Foch, then but little known in England, had been present in London at some of these conferences, where his influence permeated the discussions of the principal Staff Officers of the War Office. He also acquired even great influence over the mind of the Grand Duke Nicholas of Russia and had planned with him the opening moves of a defensive war on the Eastern battle front. . . . The German invasion of Belgium, although it made no vital difference to the resolve already taken by Asquith and Grey, preserved the unity of the nation, if not the integrity of the government."

THE ANGLO-RUSSIAN UNDER-STANDING

None of the entanglements woven in Europe during the years preceding the Great War proved to be more fateful than those uniting Russia and England. None of them was more secret. None of them seemed so unnatural. Nowhere in Europe did the Tsar's autocratic government receive such execrations as in London and nowhere were the exiles from his terrible wrath more cordially welcomed. There was of course a general rejoicing in 1907 when it was announced that England and Russia, historic enemies, had signed a treaty disposing of their quarrels in Southern Asia and delimiting their spheres of influence in Persia. Liberals, devoted to peace, retrenchment, and reform, could not do otherwise than approve. People of pacific tendencies and delusions hailed the treaty as new proof that the peaceful settlement of disputes was taking the place of the cruel arbitrament of war. Seasoned diplomats in London, Paris, Berlin, and St. Petersburg, however, knew that the treaty had an entirely different meaning and bearing.

Between 1907 and 1914 Anglo-Russian friendship was made manifest by the usual exchange of visits and speeches of felicitation on ceremonial occasions. Still it was not believed in England, outside of the government group at least, that any commitments had been made. Indeed the hatred of English Liberals for autocratic Russia was so marked that intelligent observers did not dream that the English government would favor Russia rather than Germany in the ordinary course of events. In the spring of 1914, however, persistent rumors were afloat to the effect that some kind of an understanding or alliance had been concluded with Russia involving commitments of a military character.   These rumors seemed so well authenticated that direct questions were put to Sir Edward Grey in the House of Commons.   With diplomatic correctness, Sir Edward replied cautiously that "there were no unpublished agreements with European powers apt to restrain or hamper the free decision of the Government or Parliament as to whether England was to participate in a war or not."   This was, in a formal sense of the word, accurate, but, of course, it meant one thing to Sir Edward and quite another thing to the minds of people who knew nothing about the diplomatic operations of the British government during the previous ten or fifteen years.   Such was the state of public knowledge in England on the very eve of the mighty cataclysm.

Although the English government has not seen fit to publish any documents on Russian relations similar to those issued by the French government in the Yellow Book of 1918, a great deal of light has been thrown upon Anglo-Russian relations by the new materials made public from the Belgian and Russian archives.   In these it is possible to trace with a certain degree of accuracy the policies and understandings of Russia and England between 1906 and 1914.   In the documents of the first group we have the expert opinions of Belgian diplomats stationed in Berlin, Paris, and London as to the nature and significance of the new entente.   These papers are, of course, neither Russian nor English, but they give us the sober and official judgment of informed neutrals.   They show how persons accustomed to deal with affairs of state looked upon the new understanding. They are in part founded upon rumor, but rather authentic rumor.

The first among them is a letter of May 7, 1906, from the Belgian ambassador at Paris, which throws light upon the events that led up to the Anglo-Russian treaty of 1907. It reads: "The king of England left Paris to-day after having spent five days here. . . . Some are pleased to ascribe to the presence of the king of England in Paris another object and there is reason for believing that he wishes by the mediation of France to bring about a serious rapprochement between Great Britain and Russia. That new triple arrangement, fortified by the Anglo-Japanese Alliance and by the friendship which Italy shows more and more for France and England, is already viewed, by those who love to prophesy, as an event soon to be realized and one which will assure for a new and long period the peace of Europe because Germany, in spite of the bad spirit which she may feel, cannot oppose effectively the current of ideas which now move toward that new political combination. If it is regarded as a certain pledge of peace by some, it is viewed by others as such an evident manifestation of the desire to isolate Germany that she cannot fail to search for all possible means with which to break the iron circle drawn about her."

The second document is from the Belgian ambassador at Berlin and bears the date of June 8, 1906. It reflects the diplomatic rumors and beliefs of the German capital and gives an impression of the opin-

ion current at that strategic centre. The language of
the paper runs as follows: "In spite of the friendly
discourses of English statesmen, the visit of the
German mayors, and the correctness of official relations, the attitude of the British government does
not appear to have changed since the advent of
the Liberal ministry. Sir Edward Grey assures
the public that there is no arrangement between
England and Russia, but evidently a rapprochement
is being prepared, and is already half accomplished.
Otherwise what would be the significance of the announcement of the visits of the English and Russian
fleets? Is it on account of the soundness of Russian
credit that the English market, hitherto closed
to Russian loans, has just been opened? What
can England hope or fear from a country paralysed
by long years of military disaster and by a revolution the outcome of which cannot be foreseen? As
has been said with reason the dominant thought of
the English statesmen favorable to a rapprochement
with Russia seems to be to complete and to maintain
the isolation of Germany."[1]

As to the early operations of the Anglo-Russian
entente, which grew out of the treaty of 1907, the

[1] An economic background is given in this extract from a letter
written by the Belgian ambassador in London on April 28, 1906:
"The English portion of the Russian loan has been covered in
London without difficulty by the aid of the house of Baring
Brothers. It is learned from a well-informed source that the
minister of foreign affairs, semi-officially, has urged high finance
in the capital to sustain the loan for a political object with a view
to improving relations with Russia. The Anglo-Russian entente is in the air. There is talk of mutual assurances to be
exchanged between London and St. Petersburg."

documents published from the Russian archives do
little more than illustrate what was well known
in 1914. A note written by the Russian ambassador
in London on January 28, 1909, while the Bos-
nian crisis was distracting Europe, contains a statement that Sir Edward Grey "has declared to Cambon that he wishes to inform the French government that the London cabinet has promised the
Russian government its diplomatic support in the
question of the compensation of Serbia and Monte-
negro. Grey tells me that he has taken this step in
order to clear the situation of every misunderstand-
ing. . . . The Serbian demands must be limited
as much as possible in the interests of peace."

Supplementing this note are important documents which show how Russian diplomats looked
upon the Balkan problem and especially the stroke
of Austria-Hungary in annexing Bosnia and Herzegovina. Minutes of the grand civil-military conferences in St. Petersburg from 1908 onward prove
that nothing but the low state of Russian military
forces after the Japanese war prevented the Tsar's
foreign office from adopting an intransigent Balkan
policy at once. English support had already been
offered in that connection. As weakness compelled
Russia to accept, with a wry face, the outcome of
the Austrian maneuver in the autumn of 1908, her
diplomats decided that better preparations should
be made for future exigencies. On April 1, 1909,
the Russian ambassador in Paris wrote home:
"German and Austrian journals have emphasized
the success of Austrian diplomacy and the predomi-

nant position of the Dual Monarchy in the Balkans. In consequence of this, public opinion, in France as well as in England, demands more and more a greater rapprochement between Russia, France, and England as they have already acted in common during the Austro-Serbian conflict. Foreseeing the further development of the European situation, many newspapers come to the conclusion that precisely as Germany and Austria have now achieved a brilliant victory, so must the two Western powers, together with Russia, now pay their attention to the systematic development of their forces in order to be able, once they are in a position not to fear a challenge of the Triple Alliance—and in this case Italy would separate herself from the Triple Alliance —to set up on their part demands that would restore the political balance which has now been displaced in favour of Germany and Austria. The experience of the last five years has shown that a policy of this sort need not necessarily lead to war."

In suggesting a closer agreement with England, the same ambassador gave cogent reasons of a practical kind for such a program. In a report of the same date as the above note he said: "The movement of the Central European states towards the Mediterranean is contrary not only to our own intentions but also to the interests of our allies and friends, the French and the English. The latter are particularly concerned with protecting the road from the Suez Canal to India and deem it necessary to oppose every effort to interfere with this route. . . . In view of Germany's position at Constanti-

nople, the presence of the German fleet in the
Mediterranean would be just as dangerous to Russia as was the predominant position which England occupied in Turkey, until the agreement which
you have concluded with London eliminated the
causes of possible conflicts between Russia and England. All these circumstances show how necessary
it is for us to bind ourselves still more closely to
France and England in order to oppose in common
the further penetration of Germany and Austria
into the Balkans."

The policy outlined in these notes expressed very
precisely the opinions cherished in Russian Imperial
circles. While huge sums of money were borrowed
in England and France for the reconstruction of
the Russian army and navy, diplomats redoubled
their efforts to seal more firmly Anglo-Russian
friendship. In 1912, the year that M. Poincaré
was installed as prime minister at Paris and M.
Isvolski began his remarkable negotiations with the
French premier, another Russian diplomat, M. Sazonov, undertook a delicate mission to England to
discover the temper and opinion of the English
government. The results of his inquiries he reported to his home government with full knowledge
that they would be the basis of serious and momentous steps in St. Petersburg. In one of these reports
to the Tsar, M. Sazonov thus sums up his findings
in England:

"As a general indication of the feeling respecting
Russia which I have observed in England, I must
mention that the leader of the opposition, Mr. Bo-

nar Law, was also a guest at Balmoral for several days at the same time as myself. I expressed to him, amongst other things, my satisfaction at the speech he had recently made in the name of the opposition in the House of Commons in which he approved of Sir Edward Grey's policy in the sense of a closer approach to Russia. In the presence of Grey, Bonar Law confirmed the words mentioned and in fact stated that this was the only question upon which there existed no difference of opinion between the Conservatives and the Liberals in England.

"Making use of the favorable circumstances, I thought it advantageous during one of my conversations with Grey to acquire information as to what we might expect from England in case of an armed conflict with Germany. The statements which I myself thereupon heard from the responsible leader of the English foreign policy as well as afterwards from the lips of King George himself appear to me to be worthy of notice.

"Your Imperial Majesty is aware that Poincaré during his visit to Petersburg last summer expressed to me the wish that I should ascertain the extent to which we could depend upon the assistance of the English fleet in case of such a war.

"After I had confidentially initiated Grey into the contents of our naval agreement with France and pointed out the fact that according to this settled compact, the French fleet would be concerned with the safeguarding of our interests in the southern scene of war in that it would prevent the Austrian fleet from breaking through into the Black Sea, I asked the Secretary of State whether England on its part could not render us a similar service in the north, by diverting the German squadron from our coast in the Baltic.

"Without hesitating, Grey stated that should the conditions under discussion arise, England would stake everything in order to effect the most serious blow to German power. . . .

"Arising out of this, Grey, upon his own initiative confirmed, what I already knew from Poincaré, namely, the existence of an agreement between France and Great Britain, according to which England engaged herself, in case of war with Germany, not only to come to the assistance of France on the sea, but also on the continent by landing troops.

"The king who touched upon the same question during one of his conversations with me, expressed himself still more decidedly than his minister. With visible emotion, His Majesty mentioned Germany's aspirations toward naval equality with Great Britain and exclaimed that in case of a conflict it would have disastrous consequences not only for the German fleet but also for German commerce as the English 'would sink every single German merchant ship they got hold of.'

"The last words probably not only reflect the personal feelings of His Majesty but also the prevailing mood in England with regard to Germany."

Delighted with this report on the state of affairs in England, Russian and French diplomats, as the great crisis approached, set systematically about the task of turning the understanding between Russia and England into something like a fighting agreement. Hearing of an impending visit of King George V and Sir Edward Grey to Paris in April 1914, the Russian foreign office suggested to the French government that the latter take advantage of the occasion to propose a naval understanding between England and Russia, one similar to that existing between France and England. The design worked to perfection, for the architects of the enterprise found Sir Edward Grey quite prepared to entertain the proposition and to enter heartily into the arrangement. A letter written home by the Russian ambassador in Paris on April 29, 1914, gives a full account of the transaction from the inside:

"The exchange of opinion between the English and the French statesmen dealt above all with the relation between England and France. Before entering into the exchange of opinions it was recognized by both parties that the existing agreements between the two countries required no kind of formal modification or supplement and that France and England by continuing a consistent and loyal practice of the so-called 'entente cordiale' in all political questions that might arise, would strengthen and develop the bonds uniting them from day to day. Thereby it was also acknowledged that Russia entered in the closest manner into the union between England and France as to their joint policy. This thought has been very clearly expressed in the press notice published

here and in London after the above mentioned conference. M. Doumergue told me that each word
of this notice, which was edited by M. Cambon, had
been carefully considered and revised not only by
himself but in fact also by Sir Edward Grey who
had completely approved of the mention of Russia
contained in the notice, as well as the reference to
the fact that the aim of the three powers was not
only the maintenance of 'peace,' but also, of the
'balance of power.' [1]

"After the conclusion of the discussion on different questions of the current policy that were on
the program, M. Doumergue proceeded to the question of the relations between Russia and France and
laid before Sir Edward the plans he and I had
agreed upon. He particularly referred to two
arguments in favor of a closer Anglo-Russian
agreement: (1) The efforts of Germany to
divert us from a triple agreement as being merely
an insecure and weak political combination, and
(2) the possibility of freeing a part of the English
naval forces for energetic action not only in the
Baltic and North Sea, but also in the Mediterranean. (M. Doumergue pointed out, among other
things, to Sir Edward that we would have a powerful Baltic squadron of dreadnoughts in two years.)

"Sir Edward replied to M. Doumergue that he
personally completely sympathized with the thoughts
which had been expressed to him and that he was
quite prepared to conclude an agreement with
Russia similar to the one that existed between Eng-

[1] See above, p. 18, in connection with the Russo-French alliance.

land and France. He did not conceal from M.
Doumergue, however, that not only among the government parties but also among the members of the
cabinet, elements were present that were prejudiced
against Russia and that were little inclined toward a
closer approach to that power. He expressed hope,
however, that he would succeed in inclining Mr.
Asquith and other members of the cabinet to his
standpoint and suggested the following modus pro-
cedendi: In the first place the cabinets both in London and Paris after mutual agreement could inform
the St. Petersburg cabinet of the agreement existing between France and England as follows: (1)
The military and naval convention worked out by
the General and Naval staffs, which as you are already aware, has, so to speak, a conditional character, and (2) the political agreement which is
formally sealed by the letters exchanged between
Sir Edward Grey and the French ambassador; it
is stated in these letters that in case England and
France decide upon a joint active step, according to
the course of events, the above mentioned conventions 'would be taken into account.' Simultaneously with giving this information, the cabinets in
London and Paris could ask us what our attitude
was toward the proposal relative to this action,
which in turn could give us occasion to enter into
an interchange of ideas with England concerning
the settlement of a corresponding Anglo-Russian
agreement. In the opinion of Sir Edward Grey
only a naval and no military convention could be
drawn up between us and England as the land forces

of England are allotted in advance and obviously could not operate conjointly with Russian military forces. Sir Edward Grey added that immediately upon his return to London he would place the above represented plan of action before Mr. Asquith and his other colleagues for their judgment. . . .

"All three of those present at the conference, MM. Doumergue, Cambon, and de Margerie told me that they were astonished at the clearly stated and definite readiness to enter upon a closer approach to Russia, which Sir Edward Grey had expressed. According to their conviction, the reservations made by him concerning Mr. Asquith and the other members of the cabinet have a purely formal character and had he not been convinced in advance of their agreement he would have abstained from making such concrete suggestions."

On the same day, the Russian ambassador in London wrote to St. Petersburg that Sir Edward Grey had secured the assent of the prime minister, Mr. Asquith, and a few days later added that the consent of the English cabinet had been obtained. Thereupon followed the naval conversations as arranged between the Russian and English naval staffs. The understandings existing between England and France were made known to the Russians and a program of coöperation among the three powers on the sea, in case of a common war against Germany, was worked out in the closest secrecy. This adjustment was made during the months of May and June, 1914.

Sir Edward Grey was not prepared to make an

alliance but he pointed out that no alliance existed
with France. The Russians accepted this situation,
as inevitable. On May 18, while the conversations
were being formulated, the Russian ambassador in
London wrote to his government that "even a most
careful but public alliance would meet with strong
and undisguised opposition in England and that not
only on the part of the Liberal Party, and a great
part of the political effect intended would be frustrated by it. I believe that under such circumstances an alliance would not be worth much. It
would merely in a very slight degree increase the
guarantees which are offered to France and Russia
by England and it would on the other hand offer a
far more fertile soil for agitation in favour of Germany. . . . Even those Englishmen who are firmly
convinced that sooner or later a conflict with Germany will prove inevitable would be frightened by
the idea of binding England by means of decisive
treaties of alliance which would impose obligations
upon her, the conditions and consequences of which
cannot be as yet foreseen."

In spite of the secrecy that shrouded the negotiations and the naval conversations, German newspapers, perhaps through the secret service, got hold
of the story and published a flaming account of this
new proof of the encircling policy of the Entente.
The Russian government flatly denied the allega-
tion and informed the German ambassador at St.
Petersburg that there was nothing in it. According to the notes of the Russian ambassador in London, Sir Edward Grey was "greatly alarmed by the

false rumors which were circulating in the German press concerning the contents of the alleged Naval Convention between England and Russia in connection with the question of the Straits." Sir Edward assured the German ambassador in London that the matter of the Straits had not been discussed by the two powers in five years and also assured him "that between England on the one hand and France and Russia there existed neither an alliance nor a convention." He frankly added that there was a great intimacy among the three powers and said that they had come to an understanding on all questions just as if they were allies.

As the leak made such a noise in Europe, Sir Edward Grey could not escape the necessity of facing the issue in the House of Commons. In June, 1914, he was asked point blank whether "any naval agreement has been recently entered into between Russia and Great Britain; and whether any negotiations with a view to a naval agreement have recently taken place or are now pending between Russia and Great Britain?" To this question Sir Edward replied, with great circumspection, that a similar question had been asked a year before and that the Prime Minister had then answered that there were no unpublished agreements "which would restrict or hamper the freedom of the Government or of Parliament to decide whether or not Great Britain should participate in a war. That answer covers both the questions on the paper. It remains as true to-day as it was a year ago."

The character of this reply, ingenious and careful, has been the subject of much discussion. Its technical and diplomatic correctness has been admitted but it has been suggested that, owing to the formula used by Sir Edward, his statement was susceptible of a double interpretation and that, to gentlemen who did not possess his exact information, it did not convey the same meaning as it did to its author. This, however, is a problem in ethics and casuistry. At all events as the Russian ambassador in London wrote home sometime later, Sir Edward would "find it difficult to issue a denial and go on negotiating at the same time—a rôle which he would be obliged to play towards Germany as well as towards a considerable portion of his own party and the English press." The situation was indeed delicate and embarrassing, but Anglo-Russian naval preparations were not halted by the disturbances among the statesmen and politicians.[1] When the war came a few weeks later all the two powers had to do was to order the execution of plans already prepared.

BELGIAN PAPERS AND PREPARATIONS FOR LANDING ENGLISH TROOPS ON THE CONTINENT

After their occupation of Belgium, the Germans searched the archives of that country and made public many volumes of valuable papers. One set of five volumes, composed of reports from Belgian representatives stationed at various capitals, makes

[1] For light on this subject from the German archives, see p. 72.

available a mass of secret and informed opinion relative to the policies and measures of the leading governments of Europe for many years previous to the great war. Another group of Belgian papers bears upon alleged negotiations between Belgium and England with respect to the landing of English troops on the continent in the eventuality of a war. The German interpretation of these papers, particularly the second group, has been vigorously attacked, but their authenticity apparently has never been officially denied. Indeed their authenticity is implicitly admitted by M. van den Heuvel, the Belgian minister of state, who in speaking of them declares that the papers show clearly that Belgium had no convention or treaty with England, and that she had "taken the most scrupulous care to reconcile the precautions exacted by the necessity of safeguarding the independence and maintaining the honor of the country with the duties of the strictest neutrality."

The first of these important documents, published in *fac simile* in the *Norddeutsche Allgemeine Zeitung* on November 25, 1914, was a letter from the Belgian chief of staff to the Belgian minister of war respecting his "confidential interviews" with the English military *attaché* at Brussels and with a member of the General Staff of the English War Office. These conversations dealt with the proposed disposition of English forces on the Continent in case of a war with Germany. With the details of the arrangements we are not here concerned. The point of note is that the English representative insisted on the following: "(1) Our conversation was absolutely confidential; (2) it was in no way binding on his government; (3) his Minister, the British General Staff, he, and myself were the only persons then aware of the matter; (4) he did not know whether his Sovereign had been consulted." This was in 1906.

In another one of the documents, dated April 24, 1912, a conversation between the British military *attaché* and the Belgian general, Jungbluth, is recorded: "The British government, at the time of recent events, would have immediately landed troops on our teritory even if we had not asked for help. The general protested that our consent would be necessary for this. The military *attaché* answered that he knew that but that, as we were not in a position to prevent the Germans passing through our territory, Great Britain would have landed her troops in any event."

On the basis of these documents, the Germans accused Belgium of perfidy, declared that there had been a convention or agreement between England and Belgium against Germany, and alleged that England and France would have violated Belgian neutrality if Germany had not done it. These extravagant charges were not at all warranted by the documents; and the English government flatly denied that any such agreement with Belgian had ever existed.

The English government did not however deny that "conversations" had taken place with Belgian military authorities. It said: "In view of the

solemn guarantee given by Great Britain to protect the neutrality of Belgium against violation
from any side, some academic discussions may,
through the instrumentality of Colonel Barnardis-
ton, have taken place between General Grierson
(now dead) and the Belgian military authorities
as to what assistance the British army might be able
to afford Belgium should one of her neighbors violate that neutrality. Some notes with reference to
the subject may exist in the archives at Brussels.
It should be noted that the date mentioned, namely,
1906, was the year following that in which Germany, as in 1911, adopted a threatening attitude
towards France with regard to Morocco, and in
view of the apprehensions existing of an attack on
France through Belgium it was natural that possible eventualities should be discussed."

It may seem rather strange to those unaccus-
tomed to the cautious restraints of English diplomacy that the English government should have
been officially unaware of the "conversations" in
question. From the point of view of English practice, there was nothing unusual about the matter.
The government at London frankly confessed that
such interviews "may have taken place" and that
they were perfectly "natural" in view of possible
eventualities. We are constrained to believe the
English declaration that there had been no formal
agreement and that such interviews as may have
occurred were quite "natural." We should also
take note of the fact that Lord Haldane in 1914
officially denied the German allegations and said:

"We had never committed ourselves at all to the sending of troops to the continent, and had never contemplated the possibility of sending troops to Belgium to attack Germany." Perhaps his Lordship was a bit too emphatic and sweeping when he added: "We never thought of sending troops to Belgium until Germany had invaded it and Belgium had appealed for assistance to maintain the international treaty." Possibly the contingency had been "thought of," at least unofficially, while at the same time the English government retained a free hand. Certainly the landing of troops in France had been carefully arranged.

After the war was over, Lord Haldane explained, with considerable and pardonable pride, how as minister of war from 1905 to 1912 he had reorganized the department and prepared for "eventualities" on the continent. This was done on the occasion of the coal inquiry. We may quote the questions of the Chairman and the answers of Lord Haldane from the minutes of the commission:

"CHAIRMAN. Am I right in thinking that during that time you organized the territorial forces of the crown and that also you provided for a speedy mobilization of our forces in the event of the nation being called upon to go to war? [LORD HALDANE.] That is so.

"I think, as a result of your efforts, a very speedy mobilization of our forces was effected when war was declared against Germany?—Yes. The thing we concentrated upon was extreme rapidity of mobilization and concentration in the place of assembly, and that we carried out.

"I suppose it is no longer a secret, but war was declared on Tuesday, August 4th, 1914 and I think within a matter of twelve or fourteen hours, under the scheme of mobilization which you had prepared, some of our troops were already in France?—Yes, within a very short time; within a very few hours troops were in France.

"How long was it before the whole of the British Expeditionary Force was placed in the field at the appointed place?—On Monday, August 3rd, 1914, at the request of the Prime Minister, I, as Lord Chancellor, went back to the War Office and mobilized the machine with which I was familiar. That was done at 11 o'clock upon Monday, August 3rd, and the giving of the orders took only a few minutes; everything was prepared years before."

III

DIPLOMATIC REVELATIONS: THE CENTRAL POWERS

ON the other side of the grand line-up of 1914 stood the embattled Central Powers, with Italy an uncertain factor in the background. It was known that Germany and Austria-Hungary as early as 1879 had entered upon a close alliance. It was also a matter of public record that the Triple Alliance had been formed three years later between Germany, Italy, and Austria-Hungary and had been renewed from time to time. When however, in 1916, a professional student of history, Professor C. J. H. Hayes, came to write on the Triple Alliance he could only say of the treaties which formed that association: "Their terms have never been published in full, but it is safe to say that they were defensive in character, each party promising the others military assistance against attacks by outside powers, that they were mainly directed against fears of French and Russian aggression, and that they were binding for a term of years." Critical publicists among the Entente powers, however, regarded the Triple Alliance as a mere cloak to cover Teutonic aggression in Central and Southeastern Europe, and a grand design for colonial and com-

mercial aggression beyond the seas. Such criticisms were warmly resented by the Germans whose
spokesmen insisted upon their pacific intentions.
Von Buelow, for example, declared that the Triple
Alliance was "an insurance company, not a company for profit." The veil of secrecy, if not completely removed, has at last been rent, and we can
read for ourselves the terms of the long discussed
documents.

DISCLOSURES FROM THE AUSTRIAN ARCHIVES

From the Austrian archives have come two sets of
important papers. The first embraces the secret
treaties of Austria-Hungary from 1879 to 1914.
This has been published with English translations
as well as the originals, so that American students
will have no difficulty in tracing the course of many
important international relations which were hidden from public view before 1920. The second
group of Austrian documents relates to the negotiations which took place during the weeks immediately
preceding the outbreak of the Great War. These
papers supplement and enlarge upon the materials
which the Austro-Hungarian government laid before the public in 1914 as records justifying its policies and measures. Through these papers, our
knowledge of the background of the war is immensely enriched. In them we can trace more
clearly than ever the mighty forces that steadily
converged through the years until they met in deadly
collision in August, 1914. These documents also

give us a better perspective. They remove many uncertainties. Above all do they give us an insight into the foreign policies of the Italian government and link up the entrance of Italy into the war with the policies which preceded that action.

Students of international relations, as intimated above, have known for years that an alliance had been formed between Austria-Hungary and Germany in 1879 and renewed from time to time. They have also known that a Triple Alliance between Germany, Italy, and Austria-Hungary had been established in 1882 and extended from time to time on the basis of new negotiations. These compacts were often referred to in veiled language by statesmen and debated with fervor by members of the various European parliaments, but the high contracting parties did not divulge the complete and precise terms of their agreements. "Thus," as Professor Pribram says, "it came about that on the disruption of the Triple Alliance by Italy in 1915, no one had an accurate knowledge of the tenor of the treaties, aside from the surviving statesmen and diplomats who had participated in framing and executing them: certainly an honorable testimony to the discretion of a class against which the reproach of indiscretion has so often, and not unjustly, been made." After Italy cast off the Triple Alliance, Austria-Hungary made public certain articles of the Triple compact but kept complete silence as to the remaining clauses. This was the state of affairs in 1918 when the revolution in Austria threw open the imperial archives. Although students will give thanks for the papers now laid before them for examination, they cannot forget that the whole story is not yet available. The archives of Italy and Germany have not yet yielded their secrets bearing upon the Triple Alliance. Italy has kept silent. Germany has concentrated her efforts on exposing the documents relative to the outbreak of the War. Yet the bold outline of the Triple Alliance stands clear and firm.

First among these new papers are the text of the treaty of 1879 between Germany and Austria-Hungary and certain accompanying documents. The text of the treaty confirms the assertion always made by German statesmen to the effect that it was "purely defensive" in character. Indeed the contracting parties state that while solemnly promising each other never to allow their purely defensive agreement to develop an aggressive tendency, they have determined to conclude an alliance of peace and mutual defense. They agree to assist each other in case either is attacked by Russia. If any other power attacks either of them, the other promises not to support the aggressor but to observe an attitude of benevolent neutrality. In case, however, Russia enters into the conflict precipitated by another power, both of the high contracting parties are to support each other with all available strength and to wage war together until the conclusion of a common peace. They express the hope that Russian armaments may not be menacing to them but should this hope prove illusory they "would consider it their loyal obligation to let the

Tsar Alexander know, at least confidentially, that they must consider an attack on either of them as directed against both." It is clear from this document signed just after the check administered to Russia at the Berlin congress of 1878, that Austria-Hungary and Germany looked upon Russia as the potential disturber of European peace, but at the same time felt it necessary to reckon with the possibility of an attack from other quarters. It is also clear that the document, on its face, like the Franco-Russian Alliance of 1891, bears no trace of aggressive purposes.

The Triple Alliance concluded in 1882, which supplemented, but did not supersede the alliance between Austria-Hungary and Germany, was also in its first form a defensive arrangement. The high contracting parties mutually promise peace and friendship and agree to enter into no alliance or engagement directed against any one of them. In case France makes an unprovoked attack on Italy, the Central Powers pledge their aid; the same obligation devolves upon Italy in case Germany, without provocation on her part, is attacked by France. These specifications are followed by general provisions. If any one or two of the parties, without direct provocation on their part, should be attacked by two or more outside powers, the "casus foederis" will arise simultaneously for all the contracting parties. In case any one of the three finds its security threatened by some outside power and is forced to make war on that account, the other two signatories bind themselves to observe a benevolent neutrality, each of them reserving the right to make a common cause with its ally if thought desirable. Such were the essential terms of the famous Triple Alliance of 1882. A supplementary note declared that the Triple Alliance was not hostile to England.

The first treaty was on its face a purely defensive treaty. When it was renewed in 1887 it was supplemented by special agreements. One of them, concluded between Italy and Austria-Hungary, states that, in case it becomes impossible to maintain the status quo in the Balkans, along the Ottoman coasts, and on the islands of the Adriatic and the Aegean, the two parties are to coöperate in the division of the territory, on the basis of reciprocal compensation. In a far more significant agreement between Germany and Italy, there are two astounding articles. The first of them runs: "If it were to happen that France should make a move to extend her occupation or even her protectorate or her sovereignty, under any form whatsoever, in the North African territories, whether of the Vilayet of Tripoli or of the Moroccan Empire and that in consequence thereof Italy, in order to safeguard her position in the Mediterranean, should feel that she must herself undertake action in the said North African territories or even have recourse to extreme measures in French territory in Europe, the state of war which would thereby ensue between Italy and France would constitute ipso facto, on the demand of Italy and at the common charge of the two allies, the 'casus foederis' with all the effects foreseen by Articles II and V of the aforesaid treaty of May 20, 1882, as if such an eventuality were expressly contemplated therein."

The second of the astounding articles (IV) in the treaty between Italy and Germany adds: "If the fortunes of war undertaken in common against France should lead Italy to seek for territorial guaranties with respect to France for the security of the frontiers of the Kingdom and of her maritime position, as well as with a view to the stability of peace, Germany will present no obstacle thereto and if need be, and in a measure compatible with circumstances, will apply herself to facilitating the means of attaining such a purpose."

In the renewal of 1891, the three treaties were consolidated with textual modifications. Italy's plans for action in Northern Africa were approved and Tunis as well as Tripoli was brought within the purview of the Alliance. In the renewal of 1902, Austria-Hungary agreed to a declaration giving Italy a free hand in Tripoli, and in the last renewal, that of 1912, the sovereignty of Italy over Tripoli was recognized. While taking care of her territorial interests in Africa, Italy also notified the Central Powers as early as 1896 that "she could not participate in a war in which England and France should figure as the joint adversaries of any state included in the Triple Alliance." The Central Powers, however, refused to accept this declaration on the ground that it was incompatible with the terms of the treaty itself.

Professor Pribram, the Austrian editor of the new

secret papers, in very restrained language, takes Italy to task for turning a treaty for peace and defense into a treaty supporting her imperial ambitions. He shows from the documents how the pretensions of Italy in every direction—Africa, Albania, the Balkans and Turkey—rose with the passing years and how Germany in her anxiety to keep Italy in the Alliance forced Austria-Hungary to make ever new concessions to Italian aspirations. He states that some Austrian leaders, notably the Chief of the Military Staff, opposed constant compliance with Italian demands and advocated an open break involving the settlement of their disputes by war. Professor Pribram is not sure that this would not have precipitated a general war and made matters worse, but he is convinced that Italy was a disturbing and aggressive factor. The papers at present available are used to support this conclusion. He obviously feels that Italy cut a sorry figure in the negotiations from 1882 to 1915 and then assailed her ally in the rear. It is not necessary to pass judgment on the merits of this opinion. The direction given to the Triple Alliance by Italy's demands is, however, indisputable. It stands written in the bond. Italy got support from Germany and Austria-Hungary for her imperial ambitions in Africa against France, and then after 1915 got support from the Allied Powers for her irredentist and other designs along the Adriatic. Students of diplomacy must admit that the Italian statesmen during this period rose to the opportunities before them and represented the interests of their country with a skill seldom equalled in the history of international relations.

The new Austrian papers connected with the immediate outbreak of the Great War are so voluminous that it is difficult to summarize them in a brief sketch. Though an attempt to do this is hazardous, still there are certain fundamental matters that cannot escape observation. The first is that the negotiations carried on by Austria-Hungary during the mid-summer of 1914 were shaped with regard to a large general policy and not merely with respect to the exigencies immediately at hand. This is fully demonstrated by the long memorandum, prepared with the coöperation of the Minister of Foreign Affairs and sent with the personal letter written by the Emperor Franz Joseph to the German Emperor on July 2, 1914. In this highly important document it is said:

"If Russia, supported by France, strives to unite the Balkan states against Austria-Hungary, if an attempt is made to becloud the already disturbed relations with Rumania, this hostility is not directed alone against the Monarchy as such, but in final analysis against an Ally of the German Empire—against the most accessible part of the European bloc which on account of its geographical position and internal structure is most exposed to attack and bars the way to the realization of Russia's plans as a world power. To break the military superiority of the two Imperial Powers with the aid of Balkan troops is the goal of the Dual Alliance, but not the final goal of Russia. While France seeks to weaken the Monarchy because she expects from that an advancement of her plans for revenge, the designs of the Tsar's empire are far more wide reaching.

"If one surveys the development of Russia during the last two centuries, the steady extension of her territory, and the enormous growth of her population, far exceeding that of the other great European powers, and if one remembers that this great Empire is as good as cut off from the free ocean by her position and by treaties, then one understands the imminently aggressive character of Russian policy.

"Territorial ambitions at the expense of Germany cannot be reasonably ascribed to Russia, but the extraordinary armaments and warlike preparations, the development of strategic railways in the west, etc., in Russia are certainly directed more against Germany than against Austria-Hungary. For Russia has recognized that the realization of her plans in Europe and Asia, which spring from internal necessity, must injure the most important interests of Germany and therefore must incur her unyielding opposition. The policy of Russia is determined by unchangeable relations and is therefore continuous and far seeing. The evident encircling tendencies of Russia as against the Monarchy, which involve no world policy, have as their final purpose making it impossible for the German Empire to withstand the ultimate designs of Russia and to resist her political and economic supremacy.

"On these grounds, the directors of the foreign policy of Austria-Hungary are convinced that it is in the common interest of the Monarchy, no less than of Germany, in the present Balkan crisis, to oppose seasonably and energetically Russia's development—a development that is systematically striven for and promoted,—a development which perhaps never again can be frustrated."

Such is the large background to Austro-Hungarian diplomatic maneuvers. In detail the new secret papers show the directors of the Dual Monarchy's policy firmly convinced that the murder of the Archduke was the result of a well-organized Pan-Slav plot generated in Belgrade, that weakness in this case would not only lower the prestige of the Monarchy but fatally weaken it for future resistance, that in a few years the military position of the Central Powers as against Russia and France would be materially worse, and that the immediate punishment of Serbia was necessary and could be undertaken then with more safety than in the years to come. "The crime committed against my nephew," wrote Franz Joseph to the Kaiser, "is the direct result of the Pan-Slav agitation driven by the Russians and the Serbs—an agitation which has as its goal the weakening of the Triple Alliance and the ruin of my Empire. According to all information received up to the present the bloody deed in Serajevo was not the act of an individual, but the result of a well organized plot, the threads of which reach Belgrade. . . . You will be convinced by the latest terrible events in Bosnia that a removal of the antagonism which divides us and Serbia is not to be thought of, and that the existing peaceful policy of all European monarchs will be in danger as long as this mass of criminal agitation goes on in Belgrade unpunished." So Austria-Hungary went about punishing Serbia, if not with full knowledge of the consequences, at least with an understanding that fatal things might be set in train.

It is evident from the new documents, that the Austro-Hungarian government set out on its program of positive action with the belief that it would have the support of Germany. At a meeting of the ministerial council on July 7, 1914, the presiding officer, Count Berchtold, said that conversations in Berlin had led to the happy result of assuring to Austria-Hungary the unconditional support of Germany, with all its energy, in case of a military collision with Serbia. It is equally evident that the Austrians were fully aware of the fact that their program might very well lead to a European war. Berchtold said that it was quite probable that an armed conflict with Serbia might have as its result a war with Russia. It does not appear, however, that either the German or Austrian leaders during the early stages of the negotiations calculated on the active armed intervention of England. The Austrian ambassador in Berlin wrote to Berchtold on July 12. "The German government believes that it has convincing evidence that England will not take part in a war that breaks out in the Balkans, not even if it leads to a conflict with Russia, and eventually France."

Though aware of the gravity of the situation, the Austrians were convinced that sooner or later, Russia would have her Balkan combinations completed and that they would have to fight for their existence whether they liked it or not. Berchtold said at the ministerial conference just mentioned that "Russia pursues for the present a policy, based on a long view of things, which has for its goal the union of the Balkan states, including Rumania, in order to play them off at the proper moment against the Monarchy. He was of the opinion that we must reckon with this and that our capacity to resist such an operation must steadily grow worse, all the more so as an inactive drift in things would be interpreted by our South Slavs and Rumanians as a sign of weakness and would give an impetus to the recruiting forces of the two neighboring states." This position was sustained by the Chief of Staff who said bluntly: "From a military standpoint he must emphasize the fact that conditions would be more favorable now for waging war than at some future time, as the relative weight of forces in the future would run against us." As these conclusions are from documents that were not intended for the public, it may be assumed that the diplomats and military men were speaking the truth according to their sincere convictions and not creating a fiction for mass consumption. The Central Power's had long been building up their combinations in the Balkans and had long been operating on the assumption that a crisis would inevitably come some day.   It seems pretty clear that both of them thought the hour had struck on August 1, 1914.

One more document may be taken from the priceless records of the Austrian archives.   The public was informed more than once that the Austro-Hungarian government, in waging war on Serbia, had no territorial ambitions and was merely eager to safeguard its own integrity by punishing the troublesome neighbor.   In a general council meeting the prime minister of Austria, Stürgkh, said: "Although the seizure of Serbian territory by the Monarchy is out of the question, still it is possible to bring Serbia into a state of subjection to the Monarchy by overthrowing the dynasty, drawing up a military convention, and other corresponding measures. Also the resolution of the ministerial council did not make it impossible to rectify the boundaries in the interest of strategic necessity."   The minister of war thereupon declared that he would vote for the resolution on the understanding that certain boundary rectifications, the occupation of bridgeheads, and other similar measures were not excluded. The ministry then agreed that at the opening of the war on Serbia, an announcement would be made to foreign powers to the effect that the Monarchy waged no war of conquest and did not contemplate annexing the Kingdom of Serbia.

GERMAN DIPLOMATS AT WORK

The Austrian revelations are supplemented in every detail by the papers from Berlin archives.   In addition, the latter show, as none of the other collections do, the high state of nervous tension created by the armed peace of Europe. The feverish preparations of the Russian government were construed by the German military group as implying war in the near future, and it is not surprising to find the German documents opening with Russian affairs. On June 13, 1914, the German ambassador at St. Petersburg sent home a clipping from a leading Russian journal, headed "Russia is ready, France must be ready also," and inspired by the Tsar's minister of war, General Sukhomlinov. The article recited the fact that Russia would soon have an army of 2,300,000 men as against Germany's 880,000 and Austria's 500,000 and informed France that she must furnish 770,000 through the extension of her military service to three years.

Along the margins of a German newspaper's translation of this article are comments by the Kaiser in his own handwriting. He opened by saying: "This deserves a clear, ringing answer in the form of deeds." When the Russian writer speaks of Germany's 880,000 men, the Kaiser comments, "God be praised!" When the Russian calls attention to the network of railways for the quickest possible mobilization of troops in case of war, the Kaiser exclaims: "All against Germany!" When the Russian professes motives of peace for France and Russia, the Kaiser cries: "Nonsense!" At the conclusion of the whole document, he sums up his judgment: "Well! Finally the Russians have shown their hand. Any person in Germany who does not now believe that the Russo-Gauls are not working together at high tension for a war with us very soon and that we should take corresponding counter-measures deserves to be sent to the lunatic asylum at Dalldorf." The German newspaper which reprinted the Russian manifesto had added that "Russia began her colossal armaments two years ago in accordance with arrangements with France." The Kaiser comments: "What my General Staff has steadily asserted." This document was handed back to the Foreign Office on June 15, 1914, two weeks before the murder at Serajevo.

The publication in German papers of the Russian call to arms created an immense sensation within and without official circles. The situation was fully described by the Chancellor, Bethmann Hollweg, in a letter to Lichnowsky, the ambassador in London, on the following day. Speaking of the firebrand article from Russia, he said: "The reaction on German public opinion has been unmistakable and serious. Whereas formerly, it was only the extremists among the Pan-Germans and militarists who urged that Russia was making systematic preparation for a war of aggression upon us very soon, even moderate public men are now inclined to this view. The next result is a call for another, immediate, and extensive strengthening of the army. As a result of that, as things stand with us, the competition of the navy will be awakened for it is never far behind when anything is done for the army. I add very confidentially that, as His Majesty the Kaiser has been drawn into this current of thought, I apprehend in the summer and autumn an outbreak of armament fever here.   Although, owing to the uncertainty of Russian relations, the actual goal of Russian policy can not be forcast with any degree of assurance, and although, in our political arrangements, we must reckon with the fact that Russia, of all European powers, is the most inclined to incur the risk of a warlike adventure, still I do not believe that Russia plans an early war against us.   Nevertheless, she desires—and this cannot be viewed in an evil light—she desires to appear at the outbreak of the next Balkan crisis protected by extensive military armaments and more powerful than in the last Balkan disturbance.   Whether it will then come to a European conflagration depends entirely upon the position of Germany and England."

At this very moment when the Germans were alarmed by Russian sword rattling, they were excited over rumors that England and Russia had entered into naval conversations, or had drawn up a naval convention.   The rumors were founded on fact, for the English and Russian naval staffs had, as we have seen, entered upon such negotiations in May, 1914, but Sir Edward Grey, by a skillfully worded denial, had given the world the impression that the rumors were false.   In fact the civil branch of the German government apparently understood Sir Edward's denial to mean that there had been no conversations at all whereas he had merely said, rather ingeniously, that nothing had happened to bind the hands of the government and parliament in case a war was impending.

As the Russian government declared the rumors utterly unfounded and Sir Edward made a statement that was susceptible of being construed as a denial, the German Chancellor expressed great relief. He wrote to his ambassador in London: "It is thoroughly gratifying to learn that Sir Edward Grey has challenged with decision in the lower House the rumors of an Anglo-Russian naval conversation and has also allowed his *Dementi* to be emphasized in the *Westminster Gazette*. Had these rumors been confirmed, and in fact only to the effect that the English and Russian navies were preparing for coöperation in case a common war should be fought against Germany—an arrangement similar to the agreement which England had made with France at the time of the Moroccan crisis—had this been true, then not only would Russian and French Chauvinism have been strongly excited, but there would have arisen with us a not unjustified disturbance of public opinion which would have found its expression in a navy 'scare' and in another poisoning of the slowly improving relations with England. In view of the nervous tension in which Europe has lived during recent years the results would have been obvious. At all events the idea of a common mission by which England and Germany would guarantee peace would be endangered by complications arising at any time.

"I earnestly beg Your Highness to convey to Sir Edward Grey my special thanks for his open and straightforward declarations and thereupon bring to his attention in a prudent and informal way the general considerations which I have indicated above."

The German alarm over the news of Anglo-Russian naval arrangements, temporarily allayed by Sir Edward Grey's public denials and a later denial made privately to Lichnowsky, was raised again by secret information that came to Berlin from Russia. On June 27, after reading one of Lichnowsky's reports from London, declaring the correctness of Sir Edward's position, the Undersecretary of State for Foreign Affairs, Herr Zimmerman, wrote to the Chancellor: "By this conversation [with Grey] Lichnowsky, as was to be expected, has allowed himself to be completely bamboozled again by Grey and is strengthened anew in the opinion that he has to deal with an honorable, truth-loving man. There is nothing left to do but to give to Lichnowsky some naturally quite prudent hints as to the undoubtedly trustworthy information coming to us secretly from St. Petersburg which leaves no question about the existence of continuous political and military arrangements between England and France and about the already effected negotiations between England and Russia leading to identical results."

From the German papers before us, the conclusion must inevitably be reached that while the civil wing of the German government believed in the peaceful intentions of the members of the Triple Entente, the military branch professed to believe that an aggressive war was about to be precipitated by Russia with the support of France and England and that Russia and England were actively engaged in making arrangements similar to those already existing between England and France. It is still an open question whether Russia did actually contemplate an early war on the Central Powers, but it is not to be doubted that England and Russia were in fact making arrangements for naval coöperation, in case of war, along the lines of the Anglo-French understanding. At all events when the Archduke was assassinated at Serajevo, the German Government was laboring under considerable excitement. The military group was certainly convinced that Russia was preparing to execute some plans on the field of battle.

At the exact moment when high tension existed in German official circles came the murder of the Archduke. Naturally, the Kaiser was very much exercised by the news of the affair, and he spurred on his subordinates in supporting Austria by vigorous comments on the margins of the secret papers. When Tschirschky, the German ambassador at Berlin, wrote home that apparently only young men had been involved in the crime of Serajevo and only milder forms of punishment were therefore possible, the Kaiser exclaimed: "Let us hope not." His minister had heard that there was going to be a thoroughgoing reckoning with Serbia, and he added: "Now or never." Tschirschky warned the

Austrians against hasty action; on this point the Kaiser wrote: "Who authorized him to do that? That is very stupid. It is not his business, as it is entirely Austria's affair to decide what shall be done in this matter. . . . Tschirschky should please let nonsense alone. The Serbs must be reduced to order *and* that certainly *soon*." The Kaiser vigorously objected to treating "murderers" like "gentlemen." Counsels of prudence and moderation he characterized as "imbecility" and "childish." He chafed at delays and urged Austria to carry out her plan for making demands that Serbia could not possibly accept. He declared that "the rascals had followed agitation by murder and must be humbled." He gave Austria a free hand and his unconditional support shortly after the opening of the crucial negotiations—unconditional support backed by angry and insistent assertions that nothing moderate be done. Whether in his blind rage he dreamed of all the terrible consequences to follow is not apparent, but certainly he was well informed as to the possibilities of a general conflagration. No one is more responsible than William II for encouraging Austria to light the European fire.

In the formal official papers the Kaiser does not appear as angry and petulant as in his side comments on documents sent to him for consideration. Nevertheless he was zealous in his support of Austria in her plans for punishing the Serbs, although he seemed a bit cautious at first, as, indeed, were his

close official advisers. When the Austrian ambassador called on him on July 5, 1914, William II
said that he had expected serious action on the
part of Vienna against the Serbs, but that the possibility of grave complications must be kept in mind
and that furthermore he would not make a definite
reply to the request for support until he had consulted his Imperial Chancellor. After lunch, however, the Kaiser appears to have warmed up. He
told the Austrian ambassador that Austria could
count upon the full support of Germany. He added
that while, as he had said, it was necessary for him
to obtain the opinion of his Chancellor, he had no
doubt Bethmann Hollweg would approve his position in the matter. The next day the German government officially informed Vienna that Austria
must be the judge of what should be done to Serbia
and that she could count upon the support of her
ally and friend, Germany. A few days later, in a
personal letter to the Austrian Emperor, the Kaiser
reiterated his pledge given through ministerial
channels and said: "In these tragic hours you will
find me and my empire in complete unity on your
side, true to our old and tested friendship and to
our obligations as an ally." Perhaps the spirit of
German diplomacy at this moment is reflected in a
message written in English for the Kaiser to send
to the Tsar but withheld for some reason. It ran
in part: "It is the common interest of you and
me and in fact of all monarchs that this crime and
all that are morally responsible for it should re-

ceive the punishment it deserves. Austria must be allowed a free hand to take the evil by the root and wipe out the revolutionary movement in Servia, which may, by spreading over other countries, one day threaten your throne as well as mine. The spirit of the people that murdered their own king and his wife still governs the country. It would be folly and suicidal on our part to do anything to spare them the penalty they have incurred."

This position was taken, it seems, with the thought that the conflict could be localized, that Austria-Hungary could be permitted to thrash the Serbs on her own account. It is true that the Austrian memorandum, quoted above, showing the political philosophy of Vienna in the large, was sent to Berlin. It appears among the German documents. In spite of this fact, so far as the evidence before us goes, the German foreign office was not aware of the hidden designs under the Austrian ultimatum and war policy. Neither was that office kept fully informed on the various aggressive maneuvers executed in Vienna. Taking the offers of German support at their face value, the Austrians assumed that there was no limit to the punitive measures they could take. It may be said, therefore, that the German government was not a party to all the operations in Vienna which produced the great calamity. At the same time it must be added that the German officials were aware that the conflict might not be localized, and they knew that in case it could not be, they would have to accept the responsibilities of the Alliance and the challenge of war.

The truth is that the German documents represent a confused state of mind in Berlin. Some of the officials thought that England and France did not want war and that Russia had not yet completed her military preparations, at least to such an extent that she was ready for war. Others took the position that both Russia and England were not telling the truth when they denied the rumors afloat as to their naval agreements. On one day it was thought that German relations with England were improving; on the next day they appeared to be worse. So the tide of opinion flowed and ebbed. Uncertainty reigned in all departments, until at length it became clear in Berlin that England would not stand aside and wait in case Russia and France were drawn into the conflict. That was definite at least by July 30. On that day Bethmann Hollweg transmitted to Vienna a message from Lichnowsky which proposed mediation once more and indicated that Sir Edward Grey now took a rather positive position. As if in some anguish of spirit the Chancellor added: "If Austria rejects this mediation, we shall stand in the presence of a conflagration in which England will be against us, Italy and Rumania not with us—we two against four great powers. Owing to the enmity of England, the chief weight of the conflict will fall on Germany. Austria's political prestige, the military honor of

her army, and all her just claims against Serbia
can be satisfactorily guaranteed by the occupation
of Belgrade or a few other places. By the humilia-
tion of Serbia, Austria would make her position in
the Balkans and in Russia strong again. Under
these circumstances we must invite the Vienna Cabinet, in an urgent and emphatic manner, to accept
the mediation under the honorable conditions
specified. The responsibility for the results arising from contrary action would be exceedingly
heavy."

On the day that this letter was written, the control of affairs was passing from the hands of the
civil branch of the German government into the
hands of the military division. Austria had declared war on Serbia and was feverishly carrying
forward her military preparations. By July 29,
at least, Russia had ordered "partial mobilization."
Then the Tsar, timid and vacillating, attempted to
draw back and cancel his own orders. "But," as
Professor Fay has shown from painstaking re-
searches, "the Tsar was flatly disobeyed and deceived by the Russian militarists who thereby rendered futile the Kaiser's efforts to check Russian
military measures until he could effect a settlement
by his mediation at Vienna. On July 30, the Tsar
was persuaded to approve 'general mobilization,'
thereby at last making legal and regular the secret
military measures which his militarists had disobedi-
ently been carrying on behind his back." The German military party, when news of Russian mobiliza-

tion was confirmed in Berlin, insisted that Russian
mobilization meant war and that further diplomatic
negotiations would only give the Russians tremendous advantages by enabling them to bring their
vast horde together before action was started.   At
Vienna and Berlin, events had placed the military
parties in the saddle.   Germany mobilized at once
and the issue was tried by battle.

From the facts presented above, certain general
conclusions seem to emerge.   The first and perhaps
most important is that formal treaties, either secret
or published, are not necessary to draw nations into
warlike combinations.   This may be done by "conversations," exchanges of diplomatic notes, and understandings.   Moreover,   circumstances,   rather
than the form and language of the understandings,
determine the outcome.   Italy was bound by a
solemn alliance with Austria and Germany; she decided that it did not operate, was not binding, did
not apply; she entered the war against her former
allies.   England had only held "conversations" with
France; she construed them to be "obligations of
honor" and fulfilled them.   The relations between
England and Russia were still more tenuous, but
they proved to be hooks of steel.

The second conclusion is that all the diplomats of
Europe were convinced that a general war was in the
highest degree probable and devoted themselves to
special alliances and agreements in preparation for
the terrible eventuality.

The third conclusion is that neither the members

of parliaments nor the masses of the people knew what was going on behind their backs.   Had all the records been open what would have been the result? That is the question.

IV

THE ECONOMIC OUTCOME
OF THE WAR

FOR many years before the Great War, the statesmen and diplomats of Europe pursued, let us say patriotically and honorably, the interests of their respective nations as they were given to see those interests. To accomplish their purposes, they relied upon secret negotiations, alliances, ententes, conversations, and understandings and upon huge military and naval equipments. There were some critics who protested against these methods and these reliances, but the statesmen and diplomats were above all things practical men. Their ways were old and tried while all new ways were the ways of visionaries. The practical men had their day. The Great War and its results are the· full fruit of their planting and their cultivating. The present state of Europe is a tribute to their powers of divination and to their genius for the instant need of things.

There is no doubt about the present state of Europe. Every day news, every book, every article dealing with Europe bears witness to the chaos that has followed the armistice. Statistical tables that will not be denied tell of staggering debts, mounting deficits, paralyzed industries, inflated currencies, and growing bitterness. At the end of four years of peace, Europe is, in many respects, in a worse condition than at the end of four years of war. Conference after conference has been held and the assembly of the League of Nations has convened, but these things have not brought health or understanding. In the midst of gathering difficulties statesmen are frantically talking about "restoring the economic order of Europe," "getting back to normal conditions," and "re-establishing prosperity." This is uppermost now in the minds of leaders like Mr. Lloyd George who, weary of the snarling voices of the Old World, are striving to forget the past and bring some order out of chaos.

THE ECONOMIC FOUNDATION OF THE OLD ORDER

It is fitting therefore that before examining the present state of European economy we should inquire what was the basis of the vanished "normalcy" which statesmen would fain restore. It is not difficult to find a satisfactory answer to this question. The prosperity of Europe in July, 1914, depended on the relatively free and easy operation of economic forces on a world stage—a ready exchange of commodities, unimpeded intercourse, friendly negotiations, and spirited rivalry among all the commercial nations. There were of course tariffs, bounties, monopolies, state subsidies, and other hindrances to complete freedom, but in point of fact the merchants, manufacturers, and capitalists of all countries had before them an immense and varied market for the fruits of their enterprise.

Now strange as it may seem—and this is one of the paradoxes of the situation—the most important branch of the trade of all European countries was not with the backward races of the earth which they were so eagerly struggling to conquer and hold, but with their powerful and enlightened neighbors. In 1911, for example, Great Britain, sold to Germany fifty-seven million pounds worth of goods. That was more than the value of her exports to her immense Indian empire with its two hundred million subjects. In the same year England sold to Russia goods to the value of twenty-two million pounds. That was more than she sold to all the dusky natives of her African and distant insular possessions. In 1913, England's business with Germany, counting exports and imports, was equal to more than one-third her entire business with all her colonies, dominions, and dependencies. In other words, on the eve of the war, Great Britain's business with Germany—her bitterest rival—was a vital part of her economic life. There is another fact worth remembering, namely, that Great Britain, in 1913, did five hundred million pounds worth of business with her imperial possessions and a billion pounds worth of business with the lands she did not rule, namely, the free nations of the earth. When we recall that the World War cost Great Britain about ten billion pounds and that the annual interest and other charges on her debt in 1921 amounted to three hundred fifty million pounds, we may be permitted to raise a question as to whether commercial warfare by arms "pays" in any sense of the word.

The immense trade which Great Britain enjoyed with Germany, Austria-Hungary, and eastern Europe generally was built upon the prosperity of those sections; upon a vast economic complex with centres at Berlin and Vienna—especially upon the huge net work of agencies and enterprises which Germany had constructed in all parts of the world. Even Vienna was the metropolis of a large free trade empire. It was an important financial seat with branch banks in the leading cities of the provinces. At Vienna large undertakings were conceived, planned, and executed. It was also a railway centre with radii in every direction, affording ready intercourse with the whole economic area of the empire and making excellent connections with the outside world. It fostered industries of the finer sort dependent for markets upon distant places. If so-called Middle Europe constituted a menace to England, France, and Russia, it also, by virtue of its prosperity, offered them business opportunities both alluring and lucrative.

Eastward, beyond the German frontier lay Russia. This huge agricultural country, then welded into a vast economic unity, afforded a growing market for Western manufactures and poured millions of bushels of wheat into the industrial centres of Germany and England. In 1910 Russia exported produce to the value of 1,383,000,000 roubles and bought abroad goods worth 953,000,000 roubles. Swift and direct expresses from Paris to St. Petersburg carried merchants and capitalists to and from Russia. The Siberian railway system, in process of improvement, gave constantly increasing facilities for intercourse with the heart of Asia, where virgin resources awaited the touch of western skill and enterprise. Time does not permit us to trace more closely the network of economic ties that made Europe in 1914, in spite of its shortcomings, the most prosperous section of the world, save the United States alone. Whoever has a taste for the intricacies of chess may work out the details of the great economic mechanism from the voluminous trade statistics of the pre-war days.

Of no less vital importance to the business prosperity of Europe in 1914 was the currency system which then rested upon a gold basis. The rates of exchange fluctuated but slightly. Belgium, France, and Switzerland used their francs interchangeably. The Austro-Hungarian crown was the medium of exchange for fifty million people. Within each of the several nations the stability of the currency afforded a solid foundation for business operations. Merchants could lay in stocks, manufacturers could fill their warehouses, wholesalers could count on long term market conditions. Among the several nations, the element of speculation was relatively slight. Few people bought foreign currency with the idea of holding it for a rise. The relativity of exchange values depended mainly upon the bona fide sale and purchase of goods. There was practically no element of uncertainty in the matter of currency values. Dealers in goods could look ahead for months or even years without having to take into their reckoning the possibility of great depressions or inflations in the currency.

THE ECONOMIC RESULTS OF THE WAR AND THE PEACE

Such were the foundations of world economy in August 1, 1914. Of the ruin wrought by the war itself it is hardly necessary to speak. The loss in human power was beyond calculation. The physical damage done by contending armies was enormous. For four years immense energies were turned from constructive to destructive purposes. The foreign trade of all the belligerents was disorganized and that of Germany was almost destroyed. The strains of revolution worked significant changes in the outlook and opinions of labor. Had the war been followed by an immediate restoration of the *status quo* of 1914, the process of recovery would have been slow and painful. But to the disturbances brought about by the armed conflict itself were added the profound commercial, territorial, and financial readjustments made at the peace table.

These new factors, introduced at Versailles, were not the result of accident but of policy. There was a large school of economic writers in each belligerent country who believed that the hope of their nation's prosperity lay in the destruction of commercial rivals by military force.

From the German side, we heard a great deal of

this philosophy both before and during the war. Grumbach in his remarkable collection of extracts from German sources, *Das Annexionistische Deutschland,* has convicted the German imperialists out of their own mouths. Long before the world ever discovered Bernhardi's startling thesis, Treitschke had written: "We must never become rigid, as a purely continental policy will make us, but see to it that the outcome of our next successful war must be the acquisition of colonies by all means."

After the war had been raging a year, came the petition of three hundred and fifty-two German professors demanding the annexation of a part of the French Channel coast, the seizure of the iron districts, the retention of Belgium, the occupation of a large domain in Russia, the enlargement of the colonial empire, especially in Africa, the permanent establishment of Middle Europe under German hegemony, and the collection of the heaviest possible indemnity from France. A host of German writers declared the war to be in essence a vast commercial struggle between their empire and Great Britain and called for the liquidation of the British system on the day of victory. The plan, the hope, and the will were there but fate decreed otherwise. The distribution of the commercial spoils of the world was committed by destiny to other hands, but the distribution took place.

Such theories were by no means confined to the Germans. Everyone at all familiar with English newspapers, magazines, and parliamentary speeches between the years 1890 and 1914 knows how insistant was the reiterated clamor in many quarters for protection and retaliation against German competition.   The demands ranged from appeals for high tariffs against things "made in Germany" to calls for war.   In 1897, a hotheaded writer in the *Saturday Review* voiced the sentiments of many Englishmen when he exclaimed: "A million petty disputes build up the greatest cause of war the world has ever seen.   If Germany were extinguished tomorrow there is not an Englishman in the world who would not be the richer.   Nations have fought for years over a city or a right of succession; must they not fight for two hundred and fifty million pounds of commerce? . . . . England has not awakened to what is alike inevitable and her best hope of prosperity.   *Germaniam esse delendam.*" "Sweep away the whole of the over-sea possessions of Germany, and whatever the cost of this war may be to us in men and money, we shall breathe freely for generations to come," declared a writer in the *Daily News* of August 25, 1914.   "A steady war of attrition must be waged against German commerce, finance, credit, and means of livelihood," wrote another correspondent in the London *Times* of December 13, 1914.   "To defend British industry and British labor against German competition.   To fight against German influence in our social, financial, industrial, and political life.   To expel Germans from our industries and commerce"—such was the avowed purpose of the Anti-

German Union formed under high auspices shortly after the outbreak of the war.

The victorious allies at Paris applied with a vengeance the theory that the commercial ruin of Germany would work for their benefit, and we have been able to see the concrete results of that particular economic doctrine. Since nearly all the nations of the earth had been brought into the fray against the Central Powers, the Allies were able to destroy the banks, investments, concessions, industries, and commercial agencies belonging to alien enemies in all parts of the world. Furthermore in the treaty of peace, the Allies expressly reserved "the right to retain and liquidate all property, rights, and interests belonging, at the date of the coming into force of the present Treaty, to German nationals or companies controlled by them, within their territories, colonies, possessions and protectorates, including territories ceded to them by the present Treaty." By way of supplement, the Allies took away from Germany all her overseas colonies and possessions, seized the railways and other government property, and left Germany responsible for the payment of debts incurred in creating this property. Having disrupted Germany's world-wide trade network, and having seized her colonial dominions, the Allies gave her the finishing blow by taking away from her all merchant vessels over 1600 tons burthen and half the ships between that 1600 and 1000 tons.

This is not all. German property in enemy

countries was not automatically restored at the close of the war. It had been largely liquidated, often in the interests of commercial rivals, and no general restoration could have taken place if it had been thought desirable. Moreover all the enterprises and concessions owned by the Germans in Russia, Turkey, and China were taken from them. Article 235 of the treaty also provided that German business concerns even in neutral countries could be liquidated for the benefit of the Allied powers. Thus it seems that nothing, absolutely nothing, was overlooked which might contribute to the commercial ruin of Germany. The economic foundations of her prosperity were torn away. Middle Europe was broken up and her world-wide system of colonies and trade agencies was dissolved.

It may be said that all this was merely just retribution for sins committed. Those whose minds are fixed upon punishment rather than restoration must of course be prepared to accept the consequences of their policies in the economic sphere. There seems to be no doubt that the cosmic process often departs from the rules and aspirations of the shop keeper.

The same clash over ethics and economics has arisen in connection with the next troublesome factor introduced by the Treaty of Versailles, namely, the reparations bill assessed against the vanquished. The Germans insist that they made their appeal for peace on the basis of President Wilson's principles and they have never grown weary of calling attention to the fact that he had openly repudiated annexations, contributions, and punitive indemnities.

Those who are given to viewing politics and diplomacy somewhat coldly reply that the Germans had a year and a half to leap at the opportunity of making peace on Mr. Wilson's principles but did not take the matter seriously until they were beaten on the field of battle. Still the fact stands that on the face of things the armistice was made upon the broad and general terms laid down by President Wilson, with some reservations.

It is idle perhaps to discuss the contractual nature of the terms of the armistice as a basis for the Versailles Treaty. One thing is certain and that is that Mr. Lloyd George and M. Clemenceau had no thought of offering anything but severe terms to the Germans. The former declared a few days after the armistice and long before the Versailles settlement that "all the European allies have accepted the principle that the Central Powers must pay the cost of the war up to the limit of their capacity." The latter, more given to silence, settled down in grim determination to get what he could get without resort to rhetoric. It is true that both premiers admitted for verbal purposes the principle that they were limited by President Wilson's doctrines and the armistice terms, but they found the broad generalities of both programs susceptible of generous interpretation. In the armistice provisions Germany had agreed to "make compensation for all damage done to the civilian population of the Allied and Associated Powers and to their property . . . by such aggression by land, by sea, and from the air." When the bill for such damages

was tentatively figured up at Paris it fell far short
of the amount which the victors hoped to extract
from the vanquished.   The question was raised as
to whether pensions and separation allowances
could not be included under the general terms of
the armistice.   The American experts at the peace
conference argued that such a charge was in fact a
cost of war, not a civilian damage, and therefore
could not be included in the total amount assessed
against the enemy; but President Wilson when confronted by what was called the logic of the armistice
obligations exclaimed: "Logic! Logic! I don't
care a damn for logic.   I am going to include pensions."   So pensions were included, more than
doubling the amount of Germany's bill.

Having done their best to conciliate the angry
public opinion in their respective countries by keeping to generalities, the Allied negotiators shrank
from fixing in the treaty the exact sum to be collected from the defeated foe.   They made a long
and imposing list of items for the grand account but
appended no exact figures.   This was not because
figures in abundance were wanting, but because it
was easier to agree on generalities and postpone
the evil day of an exact reckoning.   In vain did
many experts, especially on the American side,
insist upon the healing advantages of a specific
amount.   They were overborne.   The difficult
and thankless task of fixing the bill of damages was
handed over to a Reparation Commission charged
with the duty of presenting the grand total to the
German Government not later than May 1, 1921.

So for two years the victors did not know how much they were to get and the vanquished did not know how much they were to pay—a state of affairs perhaps convenient for politicians but disastrous to sound public and private economy.

Leaving out of account the ships turned over to the Allies, the property restored to occupied countries, the territories ceded, the economic privileges granted, and a few other things, the grand bill of obligations under the reparation clauses of the Versailles treaty was completed and handed to the Germans on May 5, 1921. Anticipating the difficulties in collection, the Allied statesmen provided that the total should be represented by three classes of bonds. The first class is for $3,000,000,000; the second for $9,500,000,000; and the third is for $20,500,000,000, making in all $33,000,000,000. To meet the interest and amortization charges, Germany must pay every year two billion marks gold in money or in kind and an additional amount equal to 26% of the value of her exports, subject to possible modifications by agreement.

Thus the entire bill is at last made up, at least on the face of things, but those who made it act as if they thought it could not be paid. They have provided that the last class of bonds shall not be issued and shall not bear interest until it seems probable that the interest and amortization charges can be met by Germany. How much can be collected under the export tax scheme remains uncertain. As Germany had enjoyed a respite for more than two years she readily met the first installments of the grand bill. Such is the irony of history that she was able to do this partly out of paper marks sold to speculators in the United States. How long Germany can continue to meet her successive installments remains uncertain. Perhaps it is useless to indulge in any reflections on the subject. That indefatigable student of the economic aspects of the peace, Mr. Keynes, estimates that the reparation demand, under the settlement mentioned above, will "by itself absorb more than the whole of the existing revenue" of the German Government.

When all arguments about the ethics of the reparation bill are closed there remains what Carlyle would call the immense and indubitable fact that all payments on it must be made, in the long run, in goods. Germany cannot pay in gold because she does not have it. To take away from her the little gold she has left would complete the ruin of her currency system. Germany must pay in goods, mainly manufactured goods—the very goods with which the Allied countries are already overstocked. Before the war, they were in mortal peril of having these very goods dumped on their markets at low figures. Now, if the reparations bill is to be paid, Germany must dump them free of charge. The paradox is amusing, but there it is. The claimants want to be paid but not in the one kind of coin in which payments can be made.

In addition to disturbing trade and manufacturing, the reparations requirements keep the rates of exchange in an uncertain and troubled condition.

No kind of stabilization can be attained while such huge transactions must be made—not as the result of normal trading operations but as the price of victory and defeat. Reparations, therefore, contribute to the paralysis of industry in England, France, and Italy, and make impossible the stability of exchange which is the foundation of normal business.

Commercial disruption and rivalry, heavy indemnities,—the catalogue is not yet complete. The application of the fine principle of "nationalism" has wrought a havoc in the economic texture of Europe which can only be repaired in the course of many years, if indeed it is not made worse with the sharpening of racial conflicts. Nationalism is based upon ethnic and moral considerations. It means unity and self-government for peoples akin in race and language and occupying a given geographical area. It has no necessary connection with economic foundations of prosperity. Racial unity in itself ignores such matters as coal, iron, and raw materials. It disregards the former market connections which made for local prosperity. It creates states without taking into account the material basis necessary for the life of the inhabitants, this in spite of the fact that all peoples must live by agriculture and industry.

Once established on its racial foundations, the new nation discovers how unsatisfactory are its economic boundaries. Indeed, every one of the independent nations, recently created on the principle of abstract nationalism, has discovered its economic limitations and showed a remarkable willingness to violate the principle of nationalism in efforts to get coal and other resources at the expense of its neighbors. In addition to reaching out for more territory, each ethnic unity seeks to build up its economic sufficiency by tariffs, bounties, and subsidies. The small and backward industrial countries struggle to maintain "infant industries" for national purposes and in doing this create artificial barriers in the way of trade.

The fruits of nationalism are particularly striking within the borders of the former Austro-Hungarian Empire. Efficiently operated railway systems have been broken up and reconstructed along national lines. New currencies with extraordinary fluctuations have appeared. Many of the small countries find themselves in possession of industries that never would have developed locally had it not been for the large economic complex of which the former province was a part. Hence a new struggle for markets and raw materials. New diplomatic intrigues for new balances of power have been introduced, each independent nation having its large corps of ambassadors, consuls, and ministers. Financial mechanisms such as that centering in Vienna before the war have been disrupted and local and restricted enterprises substituted. In addition, the new territorial adjustments in the interests of nationalism were carried out in such a way as to lay the germs of new hatreds by the inclusion of many aliens within the new ethnic unities.

Moreover, the brethren now united are not as

happy with their kinsmen as they had hoped to be. Although for many a long decade, orators, poets, and editors never wearied of telling the world about the splendid unity of Pan-Slavism, their prophecy is far short of fulfillment. It is an open question to-day whether the Czechs do not hate the Poles more cordially than they do the Germans. Once united by their antipathy to the Teutons, the various branches of the Slavic race, now that the old enemy is prostrate, are vigorously contending among themselves. Nothing but the fear of the return of the Hapsburgs forced the formation of the Little Entente between Czechoslovakia and Jugoslavia, with Rumania as a strange partner. Recently when Dr. Benes, one of the architects of this union, was asked whether the political understanding might not develop into a customs union, he replied: "We shall have treaties regarding tariffs according to our mutual needs." When he was asked about the export duties laid on German goods according to the adjustments under the Versailles treaty, he replied: "Germany will fall. If she agrees to pay she will fall, and equally if the sanctions are applied, she will fall. She will not go so low as Austria, because she is a much stronger national organism, but her export trade will be ruined and the mark will become of almost no value. The application of the export duty on German goods is not popular, but we are applying it. It will raise the cost of living and be a great inconvenience to many businesses which depend upon Germany, but on the other hand some of our younger industries may be helped by such a measure of protection." The Czechs even complain that the government of Poland seizes whole trains loaded with goods sent into that country, and the Poles make equally uncomplimentary remarks about the Czechs. It may be that in time these frictions will disappear. Indeed they are already being reduced but for the present they constitute formidable barriers to economic prosperity and international intercourse.

In addition to the restrictions imposed on intercourse by racial jealousies, there are the limitations made necessary by the disruption and deterioration of railway lines, roadbeds and rolling stock. European travellers who have been into southeastern Europe all agree on the general derangement of transportation. "The trains go at a snail's pace through Serbia," writes Stephen Graham. "One day we went all day and part of the night at an average of five kilometers the hour. . . . The reason is because the permanent way has been almost ruined and will need years of work upon it and all the bridges have been blown up. The train halts now and then, and then most fearfully budges forward, scarcely moves, budges, budges upon temporary wooden structures of bridges and the workmen down below seem veritably holding the bridges up whilst the trains go over them. You stop hours at little villages, the exhausted and damaged engines being hopelessly out of repair and always in repair." Another traveller, Dr. Haden Guest tells how it took him an afternoon, two nights, and one day, in 1921, to make the journey from Bucharest to Sofia—a journey that in the piping times of peace could be made in twenty hours. "And this," he adds, speaking of his tiresome trip, "is first class express passenger traffic. The goods traffic is very much slower, and months elapse before goods delivered at a Rumanian port reach their destination in the country itself. As for the ordinary postal service, no one who can find any other means of distributing mails uses it."

When to the difficulties of railway travel are added the irritating requirements of the passport service, it is clear why a merchant would rather endure what he now suffers than search far and wide for new enterprises. For hours one must stand in line at passport and consular offices to get one's document approved or stamped. Frequently one can not stop anywhere over night without reporting to the police on arriving and departing. To all this is added the vexation of spirit caused by long delays at frontiers while passports are examined and stamped by officious busy-bodies. Moreover the process is expensive, for the unhappy traveller has to pay a handsome fee at the outset for his privileges and then additional fees to the officials who spread their rubber stamp marks and signatures over the wide margins of the precious parchment.

Any one who has been through the mill, can testify to the vivid accuracy of the following account given by Stephen Graham of his adventures in passport wonderland: "In January, 1921, I took a general passport for Europe. . . . I spent a week getting visas in London. I remembered his Excellency of Greece had changed his address. When the taxi-driver had located his new office in Great Tower Street we found that he was having a holiday, celebrating New Year's day in orthodox Greek style about the fourteenth of the month. I returned in a few days' time and his Excellency was celebrating Epiphany. Next time I resolved to take a precautionary twenty minutes at the telephone and find out whether there were any other festivals on. The Poles, I remember, asked for answers to questions on two sheets of foolscap and charged thirty shillings for a visa that went out of date before I could get to their country. His Excellency of Bulgaria I made several trips to Kensington to find, and gave him up as apparently non-existent. With the representative of Latvia I had a troublous conversation and finally obtained another useless visa for forty shillings. The Germans would not give a visa as I was entering Germany from the other side. I spent about ten pounds in London merely for the application of rubber stamps and consuls' signatures. In the course of my travels that passport became an appalling wilderness of visas and remarks climbing out of their legitimate spaces to get mixed up with wife's signature and the color of the hair. The most flattering of these remarks is no doubt that affixed at Sofia's station—'Not dangerous to society.' But I had to show that passport not only to the police and military of all nations but also on entering the gambling halls of Monte Carlo on the one hand and before entering the gates of the Cathedral of Sancta Sophia at Constantinople on the other." Among the nations whose practices are thus condemned by Mr. Graham must be reckoned the United States which became one of the worst offenders in the charges made and the red tape evolved.

Any one who had the physical and moral stamina necessary for a battle over a passport did not have to fear the rigors and hardships of European travel. The effect of all these official operations on the free intercourse and travel so necessary to commercial prosperity can readily be imagined. Though some of the restrictions have been slightly modified under pressure, the main structure of the bureaucratic system remains intact to this hour. It gives employment to rubber stamp artists, it flatters national pride, and it serves to keep alive all the precious antipathies aroused by the war.

If the Great War had been of short duration, perhaps the Carthaginian Treaty made at Versailles would have produced less catastrophic results. But to the effects of the peace must be added the costs of a long and exhausting war, the increase in debts, and the derangement of the currency systems. During the four years of actual fighting, the debt of England rose from seven hundred million to seven billion pounds. The government of France owed thirty-four billion francs in 1914; it owed one hundred and fifty billion in 1918. The German national debt stood at five billion marks when the war began and at one hundred and forty when it closed, not counting obligations imposed at

Versailles. It is not necessary to go into greater detail. The fact stands out that all the belligerent nations are loaded with a burden of debt which, if it had been imposed in the interest of science, the arts, and humanity, would have produced nothing short of a revolution on the part of the taxpayers. Financiers who groaned and labored over pennies voted for education and public health in 1914 lived to sow millions of pounds right and left with lavish recklessness in a world war. When a nation is struggling for existence finance as well as the laws are silent. Only after the armistice when the nations had recovered their breath, did they realize the magnitude of their obligations. Nevertheless, if all the belligerents had set quickly to work to hold their debts within the limits of November, 1918, even the enormous totals we have just recited would not have been beyond their financial strength (leaving out of account reparations).

Instead of balancing their budgets at once, all of them, with one exception, namely Great Britain, incurred larger expenditures than before. The French government, for example, has added to its outstanding obligations since the armistice about one hundred and sixty billion francs, that is, more than its increase in war debt. In other words, the French national debt has more than doubled since 1918. It is true that a great deal of this expenditure must be ascribed to demobilization and reconstruction. Against this increase of course we must set the sums recoverable from Germany, amounts estimated at fifteen or twenty billion

francs. Even assuming that the money can be ex-
tracted from Germany, there yet remains the
astounding fact that between January 1, 1920 and
March 1, 1921, the net debt of France, after de-
ducting the German obligations, increased
39,000,000,000 francs. Recently there has been a
tendency to retrench but it makes little impression
on the mountain of debt. The French people either
will not or cannot tax themselves heavily enough to
give the government revenues sufficient for its expenditures. It may be that this process can be
kept up for a long time, assuming a proportionate
increase in national productiveness, but it would
seem that a day of reckoning must come. If the
hopes now cherished in France of making the
Germans pay all the charges laid upon them under
the treaty settlement are not realized, then some
kind of drastic financial reorganization can hardly
be avoided.

The case of Germany stands alone in many
respects, and deserves separate treatment. At the
opening of the war the financial condition of
Germany was unusually good. Unlike France, the
Imperial Government had not financed its increases
in armaments largely out of borrowings. The
huge military credit voted in 1913 carried with it
two heavy taxes, one on capital itself and the other
on increases in private fortunes. So it happened
that in 1914 while France had a debt of
34,000,000,000 francs the German debt stood at
little more than 5,000,000,000 marks. As the
German military party counted upon a short war

and a satisfactory indemnity at the end, there semed to be no reason for alarm over the financial situation. As time wore on and the expected triumph did not come, the government shrank more and more from the idea of arousing discontent by new and heavy taxes. It financed the war by floating loans and issuing paper money. The indirect taxes levied between 1916 and 1918 proved to be disappointing in the results obtained. The two great direct levies, the War Tax of 1916 and the "extraordinary war tax" of 1918 laid upon excess profits were looked upon as merely temporary and not as a means of balancing the budget. So the crisis of defeat came without finding Germany ready for it. On the day of the armistice, the national debt stoood at about 140,000,000,000 marks not counting paper money afloat. To this burden were then added the cost of demobilization and the charge for the reparations levied under the terms of the treaty of peace.

While waiting to learn the worst about reparations and wrestling with perplexing constitutional and economic problems at home, the German government allowed its finances to collapse. The national debt rose from 140,000,000,000 marks, the armistice figure, to 418,000,000,000 marks in 1920, not including the reparations bill. The mere deficit in the budget of 1921 amounted to 71,000,000,000 marks. The amount of paper money in circulation rose from about two billion marks in 1913 to more than 80,000,000,000 marks in 1921. The end is not yet in sight and the real pressure of the reparations charges is still to come. Figured in paper marks the total national obligations of Germany amount to more than seven trillion marks. Still she has been given sixty years or more to discharge her reparations bill.

The paper money disease from which Germany suffers acutely is raging in all the other countries that were involved in the war. The circulation of the Bank of France rose from 5,723,000,000 in 1913 to 37,000,000,000 francs in 1921. In the early months of 1922 the German Reichsbank had outstanding over eighty billion marks of paper notes. To the currency of established banking institutions are added the notes of local banks and chambers of commerce. There are one franc notes and even twenty-five centime notes in France. Woe to the unlucky traveller who tries to pass the currency of Nice or Marseilles in Paris. Even postage stamps were fixed inside of campaign buttons and handed out as change on the buses and in the restaurants of Paris. Notes of all colors and in all conditions of servitude, torn, ragged, and dirty, pasted, glued, and stamped by many possessors bore microbes by the billions to the innocent recipients.

The further east the traveller goes the worse the ravages. The star of the new fiscal empire makes its way toward the rising sun. Polish marks that were worth thirteen one-hundredths of a cent in 1921 dropped heavily to two or three one-hundredths of a cent in 1922. A thousand mark Warsaw six per cent. bond was offered on the New York market in February, 1922, at $1.75 but audacious buyers only cared to bid the sum of one dollar for such a treasure. As to Russia, the veritable wonderland of paper money, one hesitates to speak. The figures are so large that only astronomers can handle them with safety. Not long ago it was estimated that some printers who stole fifteen billion roubles had really got away with only $70. Czechoslovakia, the home of relatively sound finance in eastern Europe, issues marks worth less than two cents, but issues them with comparative moderation. The franc and the lire show signs of vitality, but mainly because the foreign trade of the two countries is prostrate. Three years after the close of the war, all the former belligerents of continental Europe are in far worse financial condition than on the day of the armistice.

Commercial disruption, rivalry, heavy indemnities, huge debts, inflated currencies, and nationalistic explosions—the catalogue is not yet complete. Thrones, princely houses, aristocracies, and vast economic systems have been overturned by domestic revolution. We have witnessed for the first time the seizure of a great government by the proletariat and an attempt to establish a communistic system of production. We have seen whole industries and large cities in the hands of workingmen bent upon destroying the bourgeois processes of business and government. We have seen classes that fought shoulder to shoulder upon the battle field against a common foe, turn upon each other in terrible civil war. The tide of reaction has undoubtedly set in against radical experiments. It may go far, but it has not allayed the passions and aspirations roused by revolution. European labor, though divided over matters of policy, is better organized than ever; trade unions have multiplied their membership two or three fold. It may be that labor will prove unable to establish a prosperous civilization by its own efforts; but from all appearances, labor will not rest content with the present distribution of wealth which, it alleges, has produced war profiteers at one end and slums at the other. When the lowest strata of society, speaking economically, can read and write and, through the newspapers, books, pamplets, and moving pictures, are profoundly stirred by all the currents of thought that run through modern life, it is evident that we have reached a new stage in the history of civilization. The "normalcy" of 1914 will never return again.

On top of commercial disorganization, indemnities, huge debts, inflated currencies, nationalistic rivalries, and revolutionary fevers, there came one of the worst industrial crises that has plagued Europe in many a generation. Economists familiar with the paralysis that struck Europe after the settlement of 1815 had predicted that a similar crisis would follow the close of the World War. Their predictions proved to be correct. The cheerful prophecy that every Englishman would be richer the day after the downfall of Germany was belied by events. The year following the peace saw a collapse of commerce and manufacturing in all the victorious countries. One group of figures tell the story. In the third quarter of the great business boom in Great Britain during 1920 exports, which stood at £124,000,000 for the fourth quarter of 1918, rose to £370,000,000. In the second quarter of 1921, the export trade had collapsed and the figure for that period was £141,000,000. In spite of the predictions of professional optimists, no signs of genuine recovery are yet on the horizon. France and Italy are passing through a similar crisis. Everywhere, business depression has been accompanied by its usual associates: unemployment, failures, reductions in wages, poverty, and discontent. An additional strain was placed upon national finances, especially in England, where huge unemployment benefits were paid by the government as a sort of insurance against social unrest. Months wore into years and still no revival of business appeared.

At the conclusion of a careful survey of European economic conditions, Bass and Moulton, in their important book published late in 1921, declare "that European trade this year has, on the whole, been very much less satisfactory than it was in 1920. According to the foreign trade index, Europe is not yet coming back; on the contrary, the real economic aftermath of the war is now making itself felt." These authors are also of the opinion that the present crisis is not comparable to the business depressions of previous periods when the finances and currencies of the various countries involved were on a relatively sound basis. The existing panic they regard as a political rather than a purely economic affair and they believe that "without a return of prosperity many existing European governments will sooner or later succumb under the financial strain to which they are now being subjected."

In all the belligerent countries,. agriculture, like manufacturing, seems to have suffered from a depression more or less extended. In England and Wales, the production of wheat, barley, and oats in 1920 fell back to about the pre-war figure of 1913. In 1918, the production of wheat was 10,530,000 quarters; in 1920 it fell to 6,669,000 quarters. In France where a large area was laid waste by war, the crops of 1920 as compared with those of 1913, not adding the production of Alsace-Lorraine, were twenty five per cent below the pre-war basis. In Germany where agriculture suffered none of the devastating effects of war, the crops show a decline from the high tension of war days, but taking all things into account seem to amount on the average to the normal pre-war output. The same may be said of Austria proper, although there and in Germany the situation as regards live stock is by no means normal.

Over wide reaches of eastern Europe, the output of farm produce is far below that of 1914. The ravages of war are partly responsible. To this cause must be added the breakdown of Russian economy under Bolshevik management. The abolition of private trading, as the Bolsheviki themselves admitted, had an immediate and ruinous effect upon agricultural production, and the policy has been abandoned in favor of private economy. On top of this however came the terrible famine which added to the distress of Russia.

In Poland, Czechoslovakia, and Rumania, where, as in Russia, the destruction of great feudal estates has been in progress, agriculture is in a transition stage. Impartial witnesses testify to the fact that, at least in the beginning, the system of peasant proprietorship is not as productive as that of large estates under more efficient management. The ignorance of the peasantry in states like Rumania is a handicap to the rapid recovery of agriculture and will cause a drag on progress in that field for a long time.

Such is the rather doleful picture which economists draw of Europe and we are told that the worst is yet to come. Nevertheless strange as it may appear the course of life in western and central Europe seems to the outward eye to flow along very much as before the war. The mill hands that swarm the streets of Manchester look like the people who cheered the news of Kitchener's triumph at Khartoum and the relief of Mafeking. Oxford Street and Piccadilly in London are the same, except for the veterans of the World War turning hand organs and begging coppers at the curb. Paris, a bit subdued, is still Paris. Rome is unchanged except for the new excitement made by bands of Fascisti. The cafés are crowded with soldiers while in the countryside the old men and women with their gnarled hands dig in the fields and on the hills. Restoration on the northern battlefields goes on like magic. The throngs in the beer gardens of Berlin and the coffee houses of Vienna discuss defeat instead of victory, but they are as large and enthusiastic as in the gay times of the Hohenzollerns and the Hapsburgs. Only to the eastward are there unmistakable signs of ruin and despair. But economists warn us that the peace of Europe is only the calm before the storm, that trade grows worse, that attempts to collect the indemnities will produce a crash, and that unless something drastic is done the deluge will be upon us. Their arguments seem convincing, but still their reasoning may be a delusion.

SCHEMES FOR THE RESTORATION OF EUROPEAN ECONOMY

The sickest man in Europe is no longer Turkey; all Europe is sick, and the doctors are on hand with remedies. It would take an encyclopaedia of medicine to summarize all their prescriptions, but some of the most striking may be briefly examined.

There is first of all the school of doctors who prefer to let nature take its course. They have a theory that the designs and will of man can avail little while unconscious and half-conscious forces struggling for expression may accomplish much.

Next is the growing school of French intransigents represented by Chéradame and Gautier, who roundly condemn England for betraying France into the hands of the enemy, and demand a vigorous forward policy. Gautier favors cutting loose from England and taking the Germans aside for a private conversation. He would say to the fallen foe:

"Complete and rapid reparation of the ruins in France and Belgium, in kind or in money, indemnities to the victims of the war which you have made, and finally the delivery of the armament required by the Treaty. . . . If these demands are not fully carried into effect, we have decided to employ to the limit all the means of coercion which our actual military position permits us to apply." Chéradame, who thinks that Mr. Lloyd George is in the hands of Pan-German Jews, calls for the formation of an eastern bloc against Germany and the exercise of compulsion by relentless encirclement. These plans contemplate a balance of power under French hegemony—with Germany and Russia driven into an alliance. What lies beyond almost any short-sighted person can guess.

At the opposite pole almost, are two experienced American economists, Bass and Moulton, who after a careful survey of the present economic condition of Europe, reach certain decided conclusions as to the remedies for the disease. To those who think that time cures all things, they reply with a touch of dry sarcasm, that it does—it did for Babylon and Nineveh. All minor remedies they reject. They tell us that the continued extension of American credits to Europe will not help the situation. Indeed it may make confusion worse confounded. They do not think that devices for extending our trade abroad will touch the fringe of the dilemma. They bluntly tell us that exchanges can not be stabilized until European budgets have been readjusted and until trade-balances are put on an even keel. Still more bluntly: "Foreign exchanges can not be stabilized so long as reparations and Allied debts require to be paid."

Here, then, is the bitter medicine which Bass and Moulton prescribe: (1) reparation-demands must be reduced and inter-European war-debts cancelled; (2) tariff-barriers must be reduced and government support for trade-promoters abandoned; (3) national budgets must be balanced, debts reduced, and paper money curtailed; (4) the United States must cancel the war debts, reduce armaments, lend some more money to Europe for constructive purposes, and lower its tariffs; (5) there must be some kind of league of nations to manage, in a spirit of honesty and fairness, the common concerns of the world. The United States is in a strategic position to make Europe take notice and set her house in order.

An alternative is presented by these two authors. The United States may let Europe stew in her own juice, go in for armaments and imperialism, and clean up everything in sight, now that the chief artists in that line are *hors de combat*.

Another American, a financier of large experience, Mr. Frank Vanderlip, after a visit to many European countries, has come to similar conclusions. He believes that a radical revision of the Versailles Treaty must come; and that measures similar to those put forward by Bass and Moulton cannot be avoided if "restoration" is to be effected. He suggests also the creation of an international, or if possible a super-national, banking corporation, perhaps under the auspices of the League of Nations. It would be established on a gold basis and be directed by a body of European and American financiers. It would make loans against material goods, raw or in process of manufacture, not against corporate stocks or government bonds. It would issue notes on a gold basis designed to circulate on identical terms in all countries, thus giving at least one uniform world currency. It would receive deposits and transact through its various branches a truly international business. The effect of such an institution, it is thought, would be to place the economy of all countries on a sound financial basis, leaving the currencies of the several governments to battle with fate against real money. Whatever may be the merits of this proposal, and its merits are undoubtedly great, it has against it the special interests of the various nations that would be affected by it. French, German, Italian, Polish, and other bankers think that it is still possible to drag through the present paralysis or at least postpone indefinitely the evil day of reckoning—perhaps on the well known theory, "after us the deluge."

The eminent English economist, Mr. John Maynard Keynes, who aroused the interest of the whole world by his book on the economic consequences of the peace, brought out early in 1922 a second book on the same subject entitled "A Revision of the Treaty." In this new work, he suggests four things as necessary to the restoration of Europe: (1) the cancellation of inter-allied indebtedness including the amounts owing to the United States; (2) the reduction of the German reparations bill; (3) a fair distribution of the amount collected between France and Belgium; and (4) economic assistance to the new states of eastern Europe. By this method, he thinks, "peace and amity might be won for Europe."

In fact there is a large school of economists in Europe and the United States who insist that a restoration of old Europe is impossible by purely national efforts and that it would be undesirable if possible because it would lead to the renewal of all the old hostilities and imperial rivalries which precipitated the late crisis. They insist upon the formation of the United States of Europe, and in this they have the support of the American analogy.

In 1783 our country came out of a seven years' war, with commerce, industry, finance and currency in a chaos resembling that of the Old World today. Though not as dependent as modern peoples upon foreign commerce for their livelihood, the Americans had found the English blockade, loose as it was, ruinous to their shipping and trade. The neutral vessels that plied their arts in the midst of great hazards had not been able to make up for the loss of English business. Commerce was prostrate. Industry, slight but yet important, had been either turned into military service or allowed to lapse. The artisans of the towns, even though comparatively few in numbers as measured by modern standards, suffered from unemployment. The governments of the American Confederation and of the several states were staggering under a heavy

burden of debt, domestic and foreign. The revenues of the former dwindled away as patrotic fervor
died down and those of the latter were seldom sufficient to meet the fixed obligations. The disorders
in the currency were, if possible, even worse than
in the other branches of economic life. Like all
other governments confronted by necessity, those
of our revolutionary times resorted to the printing
press. "Do you think," exclaimed one of the
Fathers, "that I will consent to load my constituents
with taxes when we can send to the printer and get a
whole wagon load of money, one quire of which
will pay for the whole?" When once this rock
of public resource was struck, paper money gushed
forth in never-ending streams. At the close of the
Revolution there was outstanding about $450,000,-
000 in the currency of the states and the national
government. When peace came at last the habit
could not be broken. It was easier to print and
borrow than to tax and collect. The printing press
was thought to be the cure for all the ills from which
trade, commerce, and industry suffered but each new
issue proved more disappointing than its predeces-
sor and finally leaders in public affairs decided that
the country would have to choose between putting
its house in order and falling into a chaos followed
by destruction. The Constitution of the United
States was the outcome of this decision.

The medicine offered by the Constitution was extremely bitter to large sections of the country and
its adoption was brought about only by the use of
the most heroic methods. But it was finally car-

ried. Under its terms a number of fundamental economic reforms were accomplished. The immense outstanding debt, state and national, was funded into one grand consolidated debt underwritten by the authority of a central government endowed with power to tax. The national paper currency, fallen into utter contempt, was redeemed at the magnificent figure of one cent on the dollar. Most of it expired in the hands of the unhappy holders. Tariff barriers erected by the states against one another were broken down and trade on a national scale made free. Measures were taken to adjust relations with foreign countries and to restore commerce to a normal basis. The states were forbidden to emit bills of credit or to make anything but gold and silver legal tender in the payment of debts. Thus there was laid out a new course based upon established business principles, and under the new order the country recovered from its paralysis and entered upon an era of work and prosperity. Still it must be remembered that the Revolutionary war lasted seven years and that the period of confusion which had followed the war continued for six years more. It was a long "critical period," and nothing but grinding necessity brought about the final coöperative effort that created the Constitution.

THE DRIFT OF THINGS

If we look beneath the schemes of the reformers, who seek peace in a kind of constitution for Europe, to the realities of Europe we cannot escape seeing

certain very striking tendencies in the practical conduct of affairs. On the side of restoration and recovery may be set many things. In Eastern Europe,
the new republics are slowly seeing the folly of
constant bickering. A score of new treaties, political and commercial, have been signed during the
past four years clearing away antagonisms and
opening the channels of trade. The Baltic states
seem to be on fairly good terms with their neighbors. Even Czechoslovakia and Austria, a few
days before last Christmas (1921), reached an accord respecting political and commercial relations.
The members of the old Austro-Hungarian empire
are learning that wrath of man produces no turnips
and that pride of race covers no nakedness. German business enterprise is swiftly building a new
Middle Europe, economic rather than political, the
harbinger of extensive industrial activity. Russia
for a long time sat in outer darkness, but as
many separate commercial treaties attest, most of
Europe seems at last inclined to renew its connections with that vast empire with its laborious peasantry and its undeveloped natural resources. Indeed, the Bolsheviki have abandoned communism as
applied to the land and are swinging toward a form
of state-capitalism which admits of private enterprise and individual initiative. Still there is politics mixed with this economics. The new alignments
of power among Poland, Czechoslovakia, Hungary, Rumania, and Jugoslavia are closely related
to the encircling policy which the French intransigents have in mind and may lead to war rather than
to peace.

In German affairs, the drift in finance and in industry is unmistakable. The democratic forces of Germany are disconcerted and beaten. The people who led the revolution thought that the overthrow of the old government and the retirement of the bureaucrats and militarists would bring easier terms at the council table. That hope failed. The Wilsonian peace was not realized, and the anger that accompanied the defeat of the peace-makers fell with terrible weight upon the leaders responsible for signing the Treaty. This produced the inevitable reaction. Taxes are never popular. Taxes to pay bills presented by a triumphant foe can hardly be characterized at all. The capitalists will not suffer the government to levy upon their huge war profits and the revolutionary working class will not endure indirect taxes. Both capitalists and laborers are so closely organized that no government dares to defy them.

The attempt to collect a heavy reparations bill in Germany by the ordinary political processes will prove extremely difficult. That truth is concretely illustrated in the tragic career of Herr Erzberger. He came to the head of the treasury several months after the November revolution of 1918 which turned Germany into a republic. His predecessors under the democratic régime had not dared to touch the problem of finance for fear of letting loose forces which they could not calculate. Erzberger, whatever may be said of his versatility and it was very great, was a man of considerable courage. He had been an imperialist in the days when victory perched on German banners. He later sensed defeat from afar and, convinced that an early peace was necessary to save the country, he took the lead in advocating a peace without annexations and indemnities. For this he incurred the enmity of many of the militarists who, defeated in their game, did not have the courage to face the inevitable. When the breakdown finally came, Herr Erzberger forged to the front. He urged the ratification of the Versailles treaty, in spite of its drastic terms. Soon afterward called to the ministry of finance, he set about fiscal reforms with a zeal that shocked the potential taxpayers. He proposed a heavy income and profits tax, an extraordinary levy on inheritances, and finally what he spoke of as "a national sacrifice tax." This last was a call upon all Germans to surrender to the state a goodly share of their private fortunes—a tax ranging from ten per cent on fifty thousand marks to slightly more than fifty per cent on an estate of eight million marks. To these direct taxes were to be added indirect taxes falling heavily upon all business and commercial transactions. Furthermore by way of a preliminary a complete revolution in the fiscal relations of the national government and the states was devised and executed.

The storm of wrath that broke when Herr Erzberger laid his program before the country was terrible. The possessing classes, capitalists and landed gentry alike, assailed it from all sides. Though it was evident that some such prodigious fiscal enterprise was necessary to make even the normal budget balance, Herr Erzberger's plans were cut down and modified until they fell far short of the object in view. The attempts to execute the laws that did get through the national legislature met with every kind of an obstacle. A great deal of capital fled from the country, the bureaucracy blocked the efficient administration of the measures, taxpayers devised new schemes for escaping their burdens, and business men resisted what they regarded as systematic confiscation. To these difficulties were added others. All the natural hatred of taxpayers for the authors of their miseries was mingled with the wrath of the militarists and landed aristocracy of the old régime. Beaten and discouraged, Herr Erzberger gave up the task, and retired only to meet his fate at the hands of an assassin. His successor, Dr. Wirth, fell back upon the good old expedient of printing paper money to pay the bills, with results already widely advertised. If such was the outcome of a sincere attempt to restore order in German finances before the imposition of the reparations burden, what is to be expected from new efforts along that line?

In casting about for a scapegoat, the Germans seized upon the authors of the Treaty of Versailles. To that fateful document they traced the origins of their financial ruin. A congress of bankers held in Berlin during October, 1920, solemnly decided that there was no salvation for Germany outide of a revision of the treaty. If they had looked eastward they would have found a country laboring under no obligations for reparations, namely Poland, with finances in still greater disorder. If they had looked at the victorious French republic they would have found deficits almost as staggering as their own. But it was easier for the taxpayers to condemn the settlement of Versailles than to make out checks for their taxes. So the world witnessed a country possessed of great industrial resources and immense private fortunes unable to pay its current expenses—a nation in which capitalist corporations were paying from ten to eighty per cent profit while the government was impoverished.

Although the Germans resent any mention of reparations, German capitalists forge ahead with more zeal and efficiency than ever in organizing their economic Middle Europe and in reaching out for world markets. The treaty of peace was hardly signed before this renewed economic activity attracted the attention of all observers. A few German leaders, like Albert Ballin, director of the Hamburg-American Line, withdrew broken-hearted from the commercial sphere while the militarists of old Prussia sulked in their tents, but men like Hugo Stinnes and the Kirdorfs, the Rockefellers and Garys of Germany, set about reconstructing the industrial life of their nation on a better organized and more efficient basis than ever. In July, 1920, the German-Luxemburg Mining and Smelting Company combined with the Geselskirchen Company creating the Rhine-Elbe-Union. A few months later this vast combination acquired the Bochum Company engaged in mining and manufacturing cast steel. About the same time the gigantic electrical enterprise of the Siemens Company was brought into the Stinnes sphere, thus fusing concerns engaged in producing raw and finished products. Then copper, brass, and automobile works were added to the consolidation. In 1921 the Stinnes trust went across the border and absorbed the Austrian Alpine Mining Company which owned the Styrian ore deposits and before the war supplied the Balkans and Italy with immense amounts of iron and steel. Thus part of the loss sustained in Alsace-Lorraine was made good, and a fusion of German coal and Austrian iron ore facilitated. Not yet satisfied, Stinnes laid hold of the wood pulp and paper industry and then having possession of the raw materials he bought up a string of newspapers and book publishing concerns. It was rumored that he had in his grip no less than sixty newspapers, powerful organs of opinion, but his conservative biographer thinks that the number probably does not exceed twelve.

Having effected a mighty combination for the manufacture of hundreds of different articles from dolls to dynamos, Stinnes created an export department in his Transportation and Overseas Trading Company. His concern was licensed "to engage in transportation of every description as well as to build and manufacture all shipping accessories whether at home or abroad; to deal in the products of the mining, smelting, and metal industries, the chemical and electrical industry, and agriculture; to market articles of every stage of manufacture, as well as raw materials of all kinds, especially, provisions and cattle products, mineral, animal, and vegetable oils, cotton and other textiles in the un-finished state, hides, jute, wood, cellulose, paper, and all products of the intermediate industries; and to engage in the reshipping and storage of all these products, especially during their transmission to or from foreign countries."

After freight come passengers. Having estab-lished the Hamburg Travellers Company, Stinnes entered into an arrangement with the Hamburg American Line, rehabilitated with the aid of Ameri-can capital, to reconstruct the tourist and hotel busi-ness. Steamer cabins, sleeping car berths, and hotel rooms were organized in a chain and operated as one system giving the tourist complete relief from all the bother of his travelling arrangements. Whether he wishes to visit the Italian Riviera or the Canadian Rockies, the Hamburg Travellers Com-pany will look after his needs and supply him with almost every thing from Westphalian ham to elec-tric lights. All this has been brought about by the wonder-working Stinnes who in the fertility of his resources and the sweep of his imagination is worthy of ranking with such men as Edward Harriman and James J. Hill.

A special feature of this new industrial activity is the formation of the vertical as well as the hori-zontal trust. The latter is a well known and well-tested organization. It consists in the union of all the industries of a given field, such as coal, steel, or electricity, in a single coal, steel, or electrical com-bination. The German magnates of the new order are not content with any such simple and relatively easy undertaking. They are bringing about vertical as well as horizontal combinations; that is to say, they are creating industrial organizations to handle goods in all stages from the mines and forests to the finished products. The same concern will mine coal and iron, make steel, manufacture electrical appliances, build automobiles and ships, and carry to any part of the world the finished articles in its own vessels, financed by its own banking corporation. Thus the profits of the special industries which constitute a tribute levied at ten or more points are abolished and the wastes of competition are eliminated. Such a company can, if it will, undersell any competitors who are sustaining corps of profiteers attached like barnacles to the various industries through which the raw materials pass. By the horizontal and vertical organization of industry German capitalists hope to outbid, undersell, outmaneuver the business men of other countries who cling to the archaic methods common in the opening years of the twentieth century. As the government owns the railways and waterways and is in point of fact dominated in such matters by industrial interests that look upon transportation as a means not an end, the carriage of freight to the sea ports is brought into harmony with the requirements of business.

It is also a matter of note that Germany has no Sherman Anti-Trust laws. Smaller business men who are not able to keep the pace set by Stinnes and Kirdorf are not permitted to run to the legislature and set loose a pack of prosecutors upon the rivals who have beaten them in the great game. On the contrary, every German government since the revolution has either been a Socialist government or one sustained by Socialist consent, express or implied. Now the operations carried on by Stinnes and his colleagues in industry are exactly those which the socialists say prepare the way for their order of things. They admit that they cannot take over and manage a host of petty business concerns with any degree of efficiency or success, but they do contend that when the industrial capitalist has brought a business to a certain degree of "maturity" it is ripe for "socialization." Therefore they welcome the establishment of horizontal and vertical combinations and do all that they can to smooth the path for the organizers of gigantic enterprizes. Moreover the system of workers' councils and economic councils, authorized by the German constitution of 1919, was created with the thought that they would bring about intelligent co-operation in German industries, educating workingmen in their sphere and capitalists in their domain, and preparing the way for a highly efficient productive organism.

Indeed this course is openly favored by a large and important school of economic thinkers, among whom Walther Rathenau and Rudolph Wissel rank high as leaders. This school accepts as inevitable and as conducive to productive efficiency the system of "collective" as opposed to private economy. Their ideas are summed up in the word *Planwirt-*

schaft, national economy scientifically planned in the collective interest. While he was minister of Public Economy, Herr Wissel laid before the country the outlines of such a scheme. There was to be a system of economic and labor councils organized to coöperate in the stimulation of industry. Certain great branches of economy, such as coal, potash, and electricity, were to be brought under the supervision of the government. The state was to take a larger and larger part of the profits of great industrial enterprises, in the form of stocks and bonds of the various companies. The industrial securities held by the state were not to be administered by a political officer but by a state bank conducted on business principles. Large funds thus acquired were to be used by the government to give employment to German workingmen. The cost of living was to be held down by eliminating the middlemen and distributing a part of the wages in the form of material goods. The right to strike was to be closely restricted in important industries by requiring a nine-tenths vote of the employees to close a shop. Finally there was to be an economic ministry free from political control.

This scheme, which made a great sensation when it was announced under important auspices, aroused an intense opposition on the part of the capitalists and the socialists. It went too far for the former and not far enough for the latter. *Planwirtschaft* still remains on paper, but it is the center of a lively and continuous discussion. Modified in some respects and enlarged in others, it gains steadily in popular support. Capitalists know that they cannot absolutely ignore organized labor and the socialists. Labor leaders are aware of the services rendered by the initiative and organizing power of the new capitalists. Both parties know that the crude and naked exploitation of the public through monopolies over primary materials is likely to bring about a dangerous situation. So *Planwirtschaft* is the order of the day—in discussions. Meanwhile German business strides forward in its seven league boots.

On all sides, German business men aided by the government have labored to restore their export business. The ink on the peace Treaty was hardly dry before there was formed a Dutch-Hanseatic League with its seat at Hamburg. This was followed the next year by a treaty with Holland which brought an advance loan of one hundred and forty million florins to German industries. German business with Switzerland and the Scandinavian countries leaped forward when the blockade was lifted. In 1920 Germany concluded commercial treaties with Hungary, Czechoslovakia, and Austria. In that year, the Czechs bought half of their foreign goods from the Germans and sold almost half of their exports to them. The next year a commercial treaty was concluded with Bulgaria, and German merchants began the restoration of their economic hegemony in the Balkans. At the same time an agreement was reached with Russia; there was an exchange of commercial delegations, with diplomatic

immunities, charged with the duty of resuming trading relations.[1] A German *chargé d'affaires* was
sent to Moscow to promote friendly intercourse.
The Hamburg-American Company and the commercial delegates of Russia formed at Berlin a Russo-
German corporation to handle the purchase of railway and steamship materials for the Soviet government. Agents of the Krupp works, now engaged
in making agricultural implements and other machines of peace, hurried to Chili while those of the
Kloeckner combination reopened their branches in
Argentine. In June, 1921, a commercial treaty
was negotiated with China and the branches of the
Deutsche Bank were opened again in that country.
The wayfarer in the streets of London who turned
from the Veterans of the World War rattling tam-
borines and begging in the streets to inspect the
shop windows could see for sale toy moving picture
machines bearing that ominous sign "Made in Germany."

While German capitalists have been driving ahead
with the support of a semi-socialist government,
England, the classic home of free trade and *laissez
faire* has been swinging steadily in the direction of
state capitalism with its usual concessions to labor in
the form of pensions, unemployment insurance, and
similar measures. In 1916, while the Great War
was still raging, the leading British manufacturers,
looking forward to the trade war after the war of

[1] The treaty between Germany and Russia announced at
Genoa in April, 1922, merely helped along a process already
under way.

arms, formed a powerful Federation of British Industries. Two years later, the British Manufacturers' Corporation, a great trade association, united with the Federation; and the consolidated society, working in close coöperation with the government, sent business agents to search for trade in the uttermost parts of the earth. In that very year, 1918, a new branch of the British Government, the Department of Overseas Trade, was created to press British commercial interests in foreign and colonial markets. With this Department were associated many British industrial leaders in an advisory capacity. The next year, the land of Cobden and Bright adopted a great system of preferential tariffs. Mr. Culbertson, of the American Tariff Commission, is quite right when he speaks of signs marking "a return by Great Britain to the policy of colonial exclusion which we had hoped had passed with the harsh days of mercantilism."

France follows steadily in the same path. Most of the war sentiment and rhetoric have been dissipated. France is now the second colonial power of the world and one of the first investment banking countries. Books are flowing from the French press recalling the ancient commercial rivalry between England and France—the rivalry that kept Europe in war for almost two hundred years and died down for a time in the presence of the greater German menace. The drift of French tariff policy is toward a closed colonial union. The French government works hand in hand with French bankers and industrialists in their search for new markets.

A very large French party dreams of the day when France may hold that dominant position in Europe and in world trade which Germany strove for and missed. What nation on the globe dares to throw the first stone at France?

Certainly the United States lives in a glass house. Our huge industrial and banking corporations are driving hard in every market. Our government modifies its anti-trust laws to give them free sway in other lands. Our government builds an immense merchant marine at the expense of the tax payers, turns it over to private operating companies, and now proposes endless millions in the way of subsidies. Our government, finding our Eastern trade menaced, calls a world conference and by brilliant negotiation forces England and Japan apart and compels the reaffirmation of the open door for China—which means in essence, better opportunities for American trade in China. Our government, with its navy and marines, helps our investment bankers collect their debts in the Caribbean. Our government gives diplomatic support to financial and commercial enterprises everywhere on the face of the earth. Foreign affairs relate principally to investments, trade, iron, coal, oil, copper, and rubber, and other raw materials.

Take a single example, the contest for new oil fields now raging among the governments of the world. As a result of a technical revolution, not less important than that introduced by gunpowder and the steam engine, petroleum has become a basic raw material as essential to modern industrial and commercial enterprise as coal and steel. Crude oil furnishes more heat per identical volume than coal. It requires fewer men in the boiler room. It is cheaper to use. It occupies less space. It is easier loaded. It leaves more room for freight for it saves about thirty per cent of the space. Merchant ships equipped with oil burning boilers can readily outstrip those that rely upon coal for fuel. The mistress of kerosene will become the mistress of the seas. Petroleum will rule the waves.

For the fighting marine, the revolution is still more important. The oil burning battleship has a far larger cruising radius and is less dependent upon coaling stations. The space saved by installing the oil apparatus, permits an increase in the weight and range of the guns used. Our Superdreadnoughts, the *Nevada* and *Oklahoma,* can outcruise and outshoot anything now upon the seas. The ships of the pre-oil age belong to the wooden hulks of Nelson's time.

War on land, as war on sea, has become an oil war. Tanks, airplanes, automobiles, and trucks depend upon oil. Paris was saved in 1914 by the fleet of automobiles that carried the new fighting units to attack the Germans from the west. Verdun was saved by the trucks which supplied men and materials after the railways and yards were bombed out of existence. Lord Curzon said at the close of the war: "Without oil how could we have procured the mobility of the fleet, the transport of our troops, or the manufacture of several explosives? How could we have carried out the necessary transport of men and ammunition to the various theatres of war? All the products of oil, gas oil, aviation spirit, motor transport spirit, lubricating oil, .etc., played an equally important part in the war; in fact, I might say that the Allies floated to victory on a wave of oil."

Owing to the high development of the American industry, the creation of a vast merchant marine, and the growth of the navy, the United States actually threatened to dislocate for the first time since the battle of the *Armada* the sea power of the world. England's battle fleet and commercial fleet rested upon coal, of which the British Isles furnish an abundant and excellent supply. England's sea-power was built upon well planned and distributed coaling and naval bases in all parts of the world. Oil, at one blow, broke up the perfection of this grand network for commerce and war. It became necessary for England to reorganize in haste her fuel technique and to cast about for future supplies in all parts of the world.

British commercial leaders, strongly supported by their government, set to work vigorously on their appointed tasks. They operated through the channels of diplomacy and imperialism and through the Shell Transport Company, the Pearson-Mexican Eagle Company, and the Royal Dutch Company. The results were astounding. To-day, England has recovered her toppling balance and remains as before mistress of oil and water. She has two-thirds of the improved fields of Central and South America and most of the concessions; she has two-thirds of the holdings in the Caribbean, and owns or controls interests in every oil field on the five continents and the islands of the seas. In this oil empire France has a province. By an agreement made at San Remo on April 24, 1920, the two countries distributed the visible and potential oil supply of the world between them, England getting the lion's share.

This places the United States with its great navy and merchant marine in a difficult position because, owing to the high rate of consumption reached in this country, the drain upon the available oil supply will exhaust our resources within a relatively brief space of time. English leaders in oil have discovered this. One of them, Sir Edward Mackay Edgar, Bart., speaking of the superior position of his country in this respect, recently remarked: "We shall have to wait a few years before the full advantages of this situation shall begin to be reaped, but that the harvest eventually will be a great one there can be no manner of doubt. To the tune of many million pounds a year, America before long will have to purchase from British companies and to pay for, in dollar currency in progressively increasing proportion, the oil she cannot do without and is no longer able to furnish from her own store. I estimate that if their present curve of consumption, especially of high grade products, is maintained, Americans in ten years will be under the necessity of importing 500 million barrels of oil yearly at $2 a barrel—a very low figure—and that means an annual payment of $1,000,000,000 per annum, most, if not all, of which will find its way into British pockets."

The government of the United States, or rather the executive branch, was quick to discover the dilemma in which it had been placed by English operations in oil. In a report transmitted from the State Department to the Senate on May 17, 1920, the policies of the English government were brought under review and a protest was lodged against them. The President of the American Petroleum Institute shortly afterward hinted in an important address that these policies were "not in the interests of the future peace of the world." To this voice of protest and warning Mr. Franklin K. Lane, then Secretary of the Interior, added his significant query: "Do such proceedings lead to peace or war?"

This protest, for the moment at least, was unheeded. Sir Edward Mackay Edgar, speaking of English supremacy and American objections, stated: "The United States experts have been well aware of this situation for more than a year. But Congress and public opinion were not on their guard. The public at large, convinced that America is an immense reservoir of petroleum and never having seen its engines stop for want of oil, took it for granted that petroleum is a product which grows naturally, like apples on apple trees. Unfortunately for them —fortunately for us—their eyes have been opened too late."

It may be however that the note of triumph is premature. England and France, it is true, have arranged between them a division of the world's oil supply. They have agreed on the methods of financing, piping, and handling the business. They contemplate reaping a generous harvest of profits at the expense of their less fortunate rivals. But if this pressure is too strong, it may force a re-alignment of industrial powers. It is not probable that the great nations will silently acquiesce in the accidents of fortune and pay an unlimited tribute to the masters of oil. Indeed, early in 1922, England made some concessions to American prospectors in the Near East and a satisfactory adjustment of the whole business was promised. Nevertheless, the affair illustrates the intimate connection between government and business, which has such a fateful bearing upon international relations.

If the last World War grew mainly out of commercial rivalry, and the weight of authority supports that view, and if we now see signs of a more intense rivalry than ever supported by all the powerful agencies of government, what then shall we say of the future, of the restoration of Europe, of a world safe for democracy, of a chastened and enlightened mankind? In the restrained language of Mr. Culbertson, speaking in the fullness of his knowledge as a member of the Tariff Commission, "if no stay is given to the discriminatory and exclusive practices which now mark the policy of almost every important nation, we shall go forward into a period of trade war and conflict from which we shall look back even upon the conditions of this day as the happy state of a golden age from which we fell."

Therein seems to be the inexorable logic of the

European problem. A new constitution of nations, a grand European league, appears to be the only alternative to new combinations, new wars more ghastly and deadly than ever. It is, however, another thing to say that the United States, enjoying the comparative security of this hemisphere, should attempt to take part in the conduct of a coöperative system for all the nations of the earth. Certainly there is nothing in the present state of Europe that gives promise of a successful outcome, even if America had the courage and the will. Perhaps if we get enough billions invested in Europe we may take a practical interest in the establishment of a constitution of law and order for her teeming millions; but a constitution without an army is only a shadow of power.

V

THE NEW CONSTITUTIONS OF EUROPE

*T*O the outward eye, the great Austro-Hungarian, German, and Russian empires, on the eve
of the World War, presented a solid front that re-
called the substantial masonry of old Roman days.
Pomp, ceremony, and circumstance attended upon
the rulers of these mighty states as upon Augustus
and Constantine. There were, of course, nationalist
rumblings in Austria-Hungary and socialist declama-
tions in Russia and Germany, but few there were
who dreamed that these solid monarchical structures
could ever be pulled down. Still fewer were there
who imagined that the time was not far distant when
all three of them would be lying in the dust. Each
of the sovereigns had an army, numerous, well-
equipped, and sternly disciplined, ready to march
to death at his orders. Police and secret agents
searched out despised revolutionaries and hustled
them to prison or exile. Those who ventured to
criticise the majesty of the sovereign, except possibly
in Austria, were in peril of the law's penalties.
Nicholas II and William II, in language befitting
James I or Louis XIV, spoke with assurance of their
heritage from Almighty God whose lieutenants
they were on earth. A few cynics laughed, but the

solemn-visaged press echoed official sentiments without question. The monarchs seemed secure in the affections of their people; a royal procession through the streets was always the signal for a demonstration and a royal marriage for a national festival. When the Kaiser celebrated the twenty-fifth anniversary of his coronation, even the socialist organ, *Vorwärts*, spoke gently of his Royal and Imperial Majesty, merely regretting that he had associated himself with the reactionaries. Not long afterward a distinguished American University president, profoundly moved by a visit to the Kaiser, declared in a burst of enthusiasm that, if Germany were a republic, a grateful people would elect William of Hohenzollern to fill the office of chief executive. And now, how the mighty have fallen!

If constitutions represent accomplished facts, then divine right and privileged classes are dead in Europe. Some echoes of the old order may be heard in out-of-the-way places, but for vast masses of Europe, kings and ruling aristocracies are symbols of a régime that has passed away. All the states that have arisen from the ruins of the three great empires are republics: Germany, Austria, Finland, Esthonia, Latvia, Lithuania, Soviet Russia, and Czechoslovakia, not to mention anomalies like Georgia and Azerbajian and Hungary. Rumania and Jugoslavia, enlarged by additions from the former Austro-Hungarian empire, retain their monarchs, but under constitutions marked by the outward signs of democracy. Everywhere, even in

Hungary, it seems, chambers of peers speaking for great landlords have been swept away. "Privileges or discriminations due to birth or rank and recognized by law are abolished," run the words of the new German constitution. "There is one citizenship in the whole kingdom and all citizens are equal before the law," proclaims the Jugoslav constitution.

By one of the strangest paradoxes of history, the Great War which was supposed to demonstrate the supremacy of the supreme masculine virtue—valor in battle—has marked the triumph of feminism in politics. It is true, the woman movement was well under way before the conflict began, but instead of being checked by war it was actually accelerated. Nearly all the new constitutions grant suffrage to women, and several of the old constitutions have been amended to the same effect. During the past few years the vote has been given to women in Austria, Czechoslovakia, Denmark, England, Esthonia, Finland, Germany, Latvia, Lithuania, the Netherlands, Norway, Poland, Sweden, and the United States. Of the great powers that took part in "the war for democracy," England and Russia have made suffrage universal. France and Italy alone remain obdurate. The German constitution, while establishing political equality, adds a sweeping declaration to the effect that "men and women have fundamentally the same civil rights;" that "marriage is based on the equal rights of both sexes"; and that "all discriminations in civil service are abolished." Divine right is dead. Though there

may be restorations, the solid structure of autocratic rule is badly shattered. The economic and
social foundations of the old order have been swept
away.

In examining the results of this great cataclysm,
for such it truly was, one cannot help comparing
them with the outcome of the French revolution
more than a hundred years ago. Until 1918, the
written constitutions of Europe were founded on
the classic model shaped by the authors of the Declaration of the Rights of Man. Complex as these
many constitutions were one deep note ran through
them all. That note is usually summed up in the
words *laissez faire*. The individual owes obligations to the state, but beyond national defense and
the maintenance of public order, the state owes no
positive duties to the individual. On the contrary,
that state is best which governs least and interferes
least with individual affairs. The rights of private
property and of free contract are inviolate, save
when due compensation is made for infringement.
There were, of course, many modifications of this
rigid doctrine under theories of public welfare and
what Americans call the "police power," but such
modifications were for the most part restricted in
character. The new doctrines of social solidarity
and social service had made little impression on
formal constitutional law by the year 1918. Judg-
ing by the written word of the constitutions the
world still stood in the year 1789.

Under the pressure of many influences, most of
them socialistic, the constitutions created during the

revolutions of our day have introduced a new concept of the relation of the citizen to the state.
What Herbert Spencer called " the coming slavery"
has almost arrived. The Russian constitution says
nothing about the "rights of man." It proclaims
only the "rights of laboring and exploited people."
There is a grand flourish about "the rights of all
citizens irrespective of their racial or national connections," but this is immediately offset by a provision that the Soviet Republic "deprives all
individuals and groups of rights which may be
utilized by them to the detriment of the socialist
revolution." The rights of private property, instead of being guaranteed, are destroyed. The
obligation to work is laid upon all citizens and there
is embodied in the text of the fundamental law the
ancient injunction : "He that will not work, neither
shall he eat." There is to be a free press and the
right of public meetings is announced, but only
for "the working people and the poorest peasantry."
The right to bear arms is mentioned, but it is limited
to the toiling masses. The propertied class is expressly disarmed. Although universal military service is prescribed, "the honor of defending the revolution with arms is accorded only to the workers,
and the non-working elements are charged with
the performance of other military duties." The
state, instead of being a mere police constable
charged with keeping order and protecting property,
becomes the master of all economic and intellectual
life. Under its iron rule, all must operate.

The other constitutions produced in our revolutionary times, bear no such heavy impress of the proletarian hand; yet all of them show marked traces of the socialist concept of society. Indeed there is a curious blending of the old and the new. The rights of man flow steadily into the duties of man. In the German constitution we can pick out the very words inserted by the advocates of doctrines diametrically opposed. The *laissez faire* school was in the convention with its gospel of economic liberty. This is what it got when it had finished with the Social Democrats and the Catholic party: "The regulation of economic life must conform to the principles of justice, with the object of assuring humane conditions for all. Within these limits the economic liberty of the individual shall be protected." Freedom of trade and industry is guaranteed, but only "in accordance with the national laws." While freedom of contract is assured, that freedom is restrained "in accordance with the laws." The right of private property is proclaimed, but "its nature and limits are defined by law." When private property is taken for public purposes, there shall be compensation and due process, only "in so far as not otherwise provided by national law." Inheritance is made secure, but "in accordance with the civil law." The clause that exalts property rights declares that they "imply property-duties. Exercise thereof shall at the same time serve the general welfare." The owner of the soil is required to cultivate and use it, and any increment not due to new labor and capital accrues to the community. Provision is made for the "transfer to public ownership of all private business enterprises adapted to socialization." The rights of labor organizations are made as secure, if not more secure, than the rights of capitalist corporations. Labor is not only recognized by the constitution; the organization of labor to participate in the control of industry is expressly provided for in an elaborate separate article.

Society is no longer viewed as a mere aggregation of individuals struggling with one another for wealth and power, protected in their possessions by the state, and without claims of right upon the community. In the light of the new constitutions, "duty" and "service" are the watchwords of constitutional law as well as "rights" and "privileges" and "immunities." The state, born of power, justifies itself by the discharge of social obligations. As the able French commentator, M. Brunet says, of the German constitution, the old doctrine of *laissez faire* has disappeared and for it there has been substituted the concept that man while enjoying a certain number of individual rights, "must place them at the service of the collectivity." He goes on to add that "in whatever concerns liberty, strictly speaking, property, the intellectual development of man, or the means of production, there is found everywhere this dominant idea of the social function of man. Individual liberties are no longer an end in themselves, nor do they constitute any longer an independent good. They are limited and conditioned by the duty of the individual to coöperate in the well-being and development of the community. They have no value and are not protected except in the measure that they serve in the fulfillment of this social duty." This is not only true in Germany where a fusion of socialist and Prussian ideals has exalted the state. It is true in the other countries of eastern Europe, even those that are more largely agrarian than the German republic. How far these new concepts will affect political practice and political ethics the future alone can determine, but there they stand to challenge the whole gospel of the French revolution.

For Americans especially and for all students of politics who once thought that the remedy for the disease of centralization and bureaucracy was offered by the federal system, the new German constitution will have a particular interest. During the old régime commentators never wearied of pointing out the rights of states and emphasizing the separatist tendencies, particularly in South Germany. Many of them flatly declared that sovereignty was not in the German people but in the Bundesrat composed of representatives of the princes and the cities. Some Frenchmen were wont to think of the South German states as ready at almost any time to break the bond that bound them to Prussia. In the structure and operations of the old system, the principle of federalism was everywhere applied. The Bundesrat, which corresponded in a way to our senate, consisted of delegates from the states and cities, and it enjoyed in the making and enforcement of laws powers far in excess of those given to the Reichstag or lower chamber. The representatives of the states in the Bundesrat were in fact ambassadors acting under instructions from their home governments and the delegates of each state were compelled to vote as a unit. The Bundesrat alone could declare war and in practice it alone initiated all the important projects of legislation. In administration, civil and military, its powers were important and far-reaching. In addition to the impress of states' rights on the structure and functions of the national government, certain of the states had special prerogatives, extending in some instances to the appointment and reception of ambassadors and ministers. There were, it is true, powerful centralizing forces at work in the old order, but federalism was deeply rooted in the entire political structure.

This system was vigorously attacked in the German constitutional convention. Some of the delegates went so far as to advocate the complete destruction of the states as such and the establishment of a unitary system like that of England or France. While these extremists did not prevail, little was left of the rights and dignities of states when they got through with their work. In the course of the revolution several of the smaller states combined; and the new national constitution made provision for additional unions and for changes of boundaries. The frontiers of the states were made mobile with the consent of the populations affected. While a republican form of government and universal suffrage were imposed upon them, the states were so reduced in power that they may be said to exist merely on sufferance. For practical purposes the division of legislative power between the states and the federal government is gone. The latter is supreme. A national council, which takes the place of the old Bundesrat, is mocked by the mere shadow of authority. The idea of giving equal representation in the upper chamber to states as geographic entities, such as prevails in the United States, is utterly rejected. It is true that the members of the new Reichsrat are not apportioned among the states exactly on the basis of population, but any discrimination that remains is offset by the fact that the Reichsrat is little more than an advisory council. It is not an upper chamber. It does not have equal legislative rights with the national parliament. It has none of the administrative powers of the former Bundesrat. It is a chattering ghost of former federalism. The government of Germany is based upon population; not on geographical and historical reminiscences. For practical purposes Germany might as well be a unitary state.

While discarding the ancient doctrine of inalienable individual rights and federalism along with it, the new constitution makers of Europe, have also refused to follow the American model in shaping the structures of their governments. Our presidential system is everywhere deliberately rejected as conferring powers too regal and too extensive upon one man—upon a single officer who cannot be called to account, during his term, by the voters of the land.

The American concept of a senate as representing

the federal principle and embodying the idea of a conservative balance in the government is likewise put aside by the new architects. Some upper chambers are left standing, it is true, but they possess no such prerogatives as those enjoyed by the senate that sits at Washington. The Germans were so afraid of secret treaties and secret diplomacy that they wrote this special clause in their constitution: "The national assembly shall appoint a standing committee on foreign affairs which may act outside of the sittings of the national assembly and after its expiration or dissolution until a new national assembly convenes." This committee is given the great powers conferred upon committees of investigation. The American idea that a judicial court can better interpret the will of the people as expressed in the constitution than a legislative body has not found general acceptance. One of the new republics, Czechoslovakia, has adopted it, but for very special reasons. Thus the pendulum in the great clock tower of time swings forever forward and back between liberty and obligation; between the individual and the state. Perhaps it will never come to rest.

Descending to particulars, we may take note of the fate which the American presidential idea met at the hands of the new draughtsmen. The new republics have titular heads who in some instances are called presidents; but when we pass beyond verbiage to reality we find that there is no resemblance to the American concept. Europe has adopted parliamentary, not presidential, government. This is not an accident. Neither is it due to ignorance of

American experience.   On the contrary, the whole
problem was thoroughly discussed in all its bear-
ings, especially in Germany.   "Many Germans,"
says Brunet, the French commentator, "wished to
establish a chief of state who could act and represent the state with the independence and authority
of a Wilson, but their view did not prevail."   The
Independent Socialists, at the other end, fearing a
Bonaparte, strenuously opposed the presidential
system.   They said that the president must either
govern in accord with the wishes of the people as
expressed by ministers responsible to the parliament, or become substantially an autocrat during his
tenure of power.   In the first case, they added, he
would be useless; and in the second case dangerous.   For this reason the Independents did not
want any president at all, but merely a council of
responsible ministers.

Between these two extremes lay the final compromise.   The German president, unlike the French
president, is not elected by the national legislative
bodies in joint session.   He is elected by the people.
He has large powers but practically all of them are
exercised through ministers responsible to the parliament.   There are a few instances in which he
may act on his own initative in collaboration with
the voters.   Under no circumstances can he exercise such regal powers as those enjoyed by the
chief executive of the United States.   When, for
example, there is a deadlock between the two houses
of the legislature, he may intervene but only to
submit the law in controversy to a popular referen-

dum. The German president does not have an independent veto power such as that enjoyed by our president. He may however place a check upon legislation by referring any bill to the voters for decision.

Thus it will be seen that the Germans sought to carry out a very definite idea. They saw that a president elected by the legislature could not fail to become a figure-head or subservient to the body that elected him. So they provided for popular election. Thus the idea of the check and balance system is introduced; but neither the executive nor the legislative department is set free to exercise its powers for a term of years uncontrolled by popular scrutiny. The president may check the legislature by submitting its proposals to a referendum. Even in this case the legislature is not without recourse against autocratic action. The Reichstag may propose the recall of the president and submit it to the people. If he is rejected at the polls he goes out of office. If the ballot is in his favor the Reichstag is automatically dissolved.

So a new experiment in popular government is made. The Germans have attempted to create "an executive strong enough to form a counterweight to the legislature and to control the latter in the name of the people without giving him a power so great that he may override, transcend, or destroy the rights of parliament and institute an anti-democratic régime." In short the Germans reject the presidential system without instituting a pure form of parlimentary government. They have created what may be called a "hair-trigger" government. In theory, at least, it is easy to force a submission of contested issues to popular vote. Whatever may be said of this, it cannot be denied that it represents democracy in an extreme form. The reaction which such a proposal would call forth in conservative circles in the United States can readily be imagined. Nevertheless, there is a point that is often overlooked: it is minorities not majorities that are radical.

While parliamentary, not presidential, government prevails in Europe, changes have been introduced in the representative idea. In the classical homes of representative government—England and the United States—democracy was working all through the nineteenth century toward a standard based on Rousseau's formula that sovereignty is in the people and that all heads are equal and for political purposes of the same value. This meant that the number of members of any particular legislature should be apportioned among geographical districts approximately according to the number of inhabitants without reference to their wealth, their occupations, or their peculiar interests. All representatives were to be elected by majorities or pluralities as the case might be. Minorities, no matter how large or important in the economy of the state, had to go without their spokesmen in the government that taxed them and interfered with their affairs. There were, it is true, exceptions to the rule and the principles were not always applied with mathematical precision; but broadly speaking this was the concept of representative democracy accepted as axiomatic—as representing the final stage in many centuries of political evolution.

No one can run through the political writings that appeared in the two hemispheres during the decade previous to the Great War without being struck by the critical note. In parliaments and outside there were lively debates over "the failure of representative government." This was the one thing on which conservatives and radicals agreed. In Europe a large number of influential publicists, of varying political tendencies, challenged the whole system of artificial territorial districts and numerical majorities. They declared that the doctrine of abstract political equality was false and in plain contradiction to the facts of modern life. That was not all. They asserted that in practical operation it was a menace to society. It placed the management of difficult and technical public affairs in the hands of politicians who, by the force of circumstances, had to be phrase-makers, rhetoricians, and "brokers in opinion." Inasmuch as anyone of the politicians, in order to accumulate the majority necessary to election, had to command the suffrages of electors holding widely divergent views, he could not escape the necessity of employing double-meaning terms and making vague promises. Such being the necessities of politics under the old system, it followed that practical men, men of affairs, could not hope to be elected themselves and were compelled to entrust the business of the state to orators whose stock in trade was high-sounding rhetoric. Such was the indictment brought against the gospel of Rousseau by those publicists accustomed to cry "a plague on both your houses."

When called upon for their remedy, the critics of representative government made this answer. They pointed out that until the modern democratic age, representation had in point of fact been based upon the idea of drawing into the work of government men from every class, order, or estate. The old French national assembly represented the clergy, nobility, and the third estate. The Swedish parliament, until 1866, spoke for the nobility, clergy, burghers, and peasants. The English parliament from mediaeval times until the advent of democracy represented the nobility, clergy, landed gentry, and the burgesses. The remedy for Rousseau's disease, the critics said, was to apply again the old idea in a new form and summon to the management of public affairs the representatives of industry, commerce, business, professions, crafts, and other orders of society.

When they were called upon, however, to elaborate their scheme, the critics found considerable embarrassment. The old rules of law that sharply divided society into economic classes had disappeared; and while it was easy to show from the census returns that there were so many peasants, so many merchants, and so many workingmen, it was impossible to draw the lines between them and to force all of them into a few distinct economic categories. Moreover, it was extremely difficult to work out any distribution of representatives among the various orders that would be generally acceptable. For various reasons no practical attempts were ever made to reëstablish representative government along occupational lines. Advocates of proportional representation argued, however, that their proposal allowed citizens to group themselves naturally and voluntarily according to their vocational interests, if they so desired, without at the same time introducing rigid class divisions or violating the accepted principle of political equality.

Debate over representative government was in a purely academic stage when revolution broke in upon mankind in 1917 and 1918. Owing to peculiar circumstances, the revolution both in Russia and Germany took a course that had a direct bearing upon the idea of representation. In both countries in the first instance, power was seized by provisional governments when the old régime collapsed. This was true to form, for democratic revolutions had usually proceeded along a similar course. The next step would have been a national assembly of some kind to begin the new legal order. In Russia, however, the provisional government created by the first revolution showed no particular hurry in appealing to the people, and before it got a national assembly in working order it was overthrown by a radical party which completely rejected political democracy of the old type. Indeed side by side with the provisional government there had existed from the first days of the revolution in Russia a soldiers, peasants, and workers council speaking in the name of these interests and sharing the sovereignty of the state. This was the organ which the Bolsheviki used. Bent upon an economic revolution, they declared that the end justified the means and so they cast aside representative government of the old type and instituted class government operating through an elaborate system of peasants and workers councils. Putting the economic revolution first they chose the means which they deemed best fitted to realize it—namely the dictatorship of the proletariat. They thrust aside parliamentary government and majority rule—those "bourgeois devices," as they were pleased to term such instruments of political democracy. To this day they have managed to hold to power by methods so well known as to call for no comment.

In Germany as in Russia, the revolution was effected through the agency of soldiers and workers councils which sprang up like magic in the industrial cities during the early days of November, 1918. This uprising was undoubtedly engineered by the Independent Socialists whose leader, Ernest Daumig, had visited Moscow and studied the methods of the Bolsheviki on the ground. So powerful did the workers and soldiers council become in Berlin that the provisional government of Social Democrats, to whom Prince Max turned over the reins of authority, had to come to terms with the extremists.

For a time the control of affairs was vested in the hands of a joint committee representing the two wings of socialism, one of which openly advocated following the Russian example with modifications. For a few weeks these two factions in common council wrangled and debated, the Independents seeking to postpone indefinitely the calling of a national assembly elected on the basis of universal suffrage. In the end the conservative wing triumphed. On December 19, 1918, at a convention of delegates from the councils that had risen in all parts of Germany, it was decided to summon a national assembly to determine the future constitution of Germany.

Having lost this battle and having failed to elect many delegates to the new assembly, the radicals nevertheless proposed in the constitutional convention to substitute a system of soviets or workers councils for the parliamentary régime. Still the conservative Social Democrats utterly rejected the idea. The Scheidemann cabinet in January, 1919 officially declared against the council system, and announced that it would not permit the introduction of the scheme into the constitution. A few weeks later, however, there came a wide-spread strike and a committee of the strikers delivered an ultimatum to Scheidemann calling for "the anchorage of the councils in the constitution." The cabinet yielded and a compromise provision was inserted in the fundamental law of Germany.

The system instituted by this compromise is far different from the Russian model or the scheme proposed by the Independent Socialists. The political and representative parliament is retained and endowed with complete sovereignty. There is instituted however, along with it, a double set of economic councils. The constitution declares that "wage earners and salaried employees are quali-

fied to co-operate on equal terms with employers in
the regulation of wages and working conditions, as
well as in the entire economic development of productive forces. The organization on both sides and
the agreements between them will be recognized."

In accordance with constitutional provisions and
statutory enactment, an elaborate set of economic
councils was instituted in Germany. The employees
of all factories of any size are organized, beginning
at the bottom with the factory councils and rising
to a grand organization known as the national
workers council. Parallel to this organization of
employees is a system of economic councils, composed
of representatives of employers, employees, and
other interested classes of the population. These
economic councils are formed on a district basis and
are crowned by a national economic council. When
the first session of this national economic council
was held, on June 30, 1920, enthusiasts declared
that the council included in its membership the ablest
business men and labor leaders in the country and
would inevitably become in the course of time a
genuine economic parliament absorbing the sovereignty of the two political assemblies, the Reichstag
and the Reichsrat. This prediction has not been
fulfilled and indeed the signs are now all to the contrary. Most of the active workers prefer their
regular trade unions to official factory councils and
most employers prefer operating as a class rather
than as members of a grand economic parliament.

This does not mean, however, that economic influences have been withdrawn and that the political

government is supreme. The employers of Germany are independently organized in a Federation of German Industries and the employees are equally well organized in their Federation of Trade Unions. When in March, 1920, the old military party attempted its coup d' état, the political government, frightened and powerless, fled from Berlin under the cover of darkness. Nothing but a swift and deadly general strike of the workers paralyzed the counter-revolutionary action of Kapp and Lütt-witz. On this occasion the political government owed its very existence to an economic organization.

Later in 1921 when the political government was wrestling with the thorny problem of money for indemnities, the capitalists, speaking through their Federation, laid down the terms and conditions on which they would grant their economic support. This amounted in effect to a capitalist dictatorship for the moment. The ire of the working classes was now aroused. Speaking through their Federation of Trade Unions they called upon the political government to "reject unconditionally the demands made by the industrialists." Threatened by economic paralysis from the side of the capitalists and financiers and a general strike from the side of the working classes, the political government of Germany was in doubt as to which way to turn. For the moment, it seems that the promise of reconciliation and gradual evolution into a new industrial democracy offered by the system of councils has vanished and warfare along the old lines is restored.

Between the two opposing forces and confronted by the demand for reparations, the government of Germany is probably the weakest in the world.

In the midst of the changing currents of European politics it is difficult to discover tendencies that give promise of permanence, but it seems established beyond a doubt that the enthusiasm for economic councils is on the wane. It was found by experience that economic as well as political assemblies were given to rhetoric and did not produce wheat or shoes. Broadly speaking, therefore, we may say that outside of Russia the general drift of things is toward parliamentary government modelled on British lines. Economic councils still exist and may yet play an important rôle, but it does not appear that they give promise of superseding political councils.

There is, however, this important development to note. The principle of proportional representation has received a remarkable extension during the past five years. The German constitution provides that representatives in the national parliament shall be elected "in accordance with the principles of proportional representation." A subsequent law elaborates the details. France, Belgium, Norway, Finland, Latvia, Esthonia, and Czechoslovakia have adopted the device in one form or another and Jugoslavia assures representation to minorities. This system, as pointed out above, makes possible groupings of voters along economic lines, and in its pure form assures to each group a number of representatives proportioned to its strength at the polls. In practice the election results under proportional representation are in rough accord with the principle of group representation, but while economic groups as such are thus drawn into the political parliament, economic conflicts are by no means eliminated. In Germany, with proportional representation strictly applied and with economic councils elaborately organized, the old antagonism between organized capital and organized labor is by no means abated. Indeed it appears to grow in intensity. So it seems that men may rouse from their slumbers and shake their chains to earth like dew only to find in the rights of self-government problems more baffling than those of old faced by kings, lords, and priests.

VI

THE RUSSIAN REVOLUTION

IT is hazardous to weigh current events in the scales of the future but there is good reason for thinking that the historian of the next century will count the Russian revolution among the most significant acts in the great drama of the present age. There has been no social convulsion like it since ancient times when victors utterly destroyed the vanquished as Rome ravaged Carthage. The process was so terrible and so deep-penetrating that no imaginable restoration could wipe out the ruin wrought in the old order of things. The economic system which it challenged may be in a great measure reëstablished; indeed this seems to be coming about, but the open renunciation of imperialism and the revelations of the old diplomatic methods will stand among the historic events of our epoch. The English revolution of the seventeenth century, as Macaulay has pointed out in one of his best passages, was a superficial affair compared with the wide-sweeping and devastating holocaust known as the French revolution. If one had the gifts of Macaulay, one could draw comparison equally striking between the French upheaval with its Dantons and Robespierres and the Russian holocaust with its Lenins and Trotzkys.

In both of these revolutions, an old and powerful monarchy was extirpated, a church disestablished, a clergy overthrown, a nobility subverted, an immense amount of property confiscated, a flood of paper money turned loose only to be repudiated, and an ancient order of thought and economy challenged and defied. But the French revolution wrought no such havoc in the ranks of the clergy and nobility as the Russian revolution has brought to pass. The French radicals left the clergy with large revenues from the state and they firmly fixed the rights of private property in land at the very moment when they overthrew the church and dissolved feudal obligations. Though in the days of the Terror, the Paris proletariat made itself felt in the councils of state, the final outcome was a triumph for the bourgeoisie, a class with experience in the management of property and the direction of affairs, if not skilled in the arts of government. In Russia on the other hand, the power of the state passed into the control of a laboring class that had not the slightest familiarity, through practice, with the exigencies of government. Moreover that class not merely seized the trappings of the state; it assumed responsibility for the administration of the complicated organism of industry, transportation, and agriculture. It professed a desire and attempted in fact to destroy the upper classes root and branch.

As Macaulay wrote of the returning French princes in 1815, so one might write of the emigrants after a possible restoration in Russia: "They came back to a land in which they could recognize nothing.

The seven sleepers of the legend who closed their eyes when the Pagans were persecuting Christians and woke when the Christians were persecuting each other, did not find themselves in a world so completely new to them.   Events had come thick and fast.   Twenty years had done the work of twenty generations.   The old institutions and the old feelings had been torn up by the roots. . . . The revolution in the laws and in the form of government was but an outward sign of that mightier revolution which had taken place in the heart and brain of the people."   Communism is an admitted failure in agriculture.   A form of state capitalism is in process of establishment.   But the days of the Romanovs and Stolypins are no more likely to return than the days of the Bourbons and Richelieus.

It is not merely as one of the great cataclysms of history that the Russian revolution arrests our attention.   There are lessons in it, no doubt, for all those who have occasion to deal with human nature in politics, but there are more practical reasons for seeking to discover its underlying forces.   The relations of the United States to the Russian government are as yet undetermined; they are in a state of flux.   We have moved from armed intervention to homiletic reviews and are still in motion.   If the Russian revolution was brought about by a handful of agitators bought by German gold, then one policy seems appropriate.   If it was effected by a few designing men who imposed their will upon more than a hundred million Russians against all popular interests and feelings, then another policy seems appropriate.   If there is a class in Russia, now oppressed, that is strong enough and intelligent enough to supersede the existing government, then still a third policy might be adopted.   Conceivably the policy of non-intervention might be followed but that does not seem to fit in with the temper and methods of the new epoch in our history.

At all events those citizens who want to see things as they really are will try to penetrate the mists that surround the Russian situation and find out why the present group of men came to power and how they have managed to hold it.   The following pages are built, not upon the frothy essays of frenzied propagandists, but upon the soberest accounts given by Bolshevik and anti-Bolshevik writers.   In them an attempt is made to discover the nature of the forces which precipitated the Bolshevik revolution and have kept its authors so long in authority.

Until they were actually charged with the responsibilities of administration, the Bolsheviki had given little or no attention to the actualities of their communist designs; that is, to the technical questions of production and distribution.   Their leaders had written scores of books and pamphlets on the evolution of capitalism, on the state, on agriculture, and on economics, Marxian and orthodox; but they considered it academic for a small and obscure minority of revolutionaries to consider in detail what they would actually do when they grasped the reins of authority.   Their one and fundamental aim was the conquest of power—the possession of the agencies of the state; namely, the army, the police, the public

buildings, the railways, and other outward signs of
government.

This is evident from the writings of the leaders
themselves. A glimpse into the psychology of revolution is given us by Zinoviev in his little booklet on
the life and work of Lenin. He tells us that it
was customary for simple-minded labor members of
the Duma to go to Lenin for advice and counsel during the winter of 1911-12. One of them on a certain occasion said to Lenin: "We want to engage
in serious legislative work; we want to consult you
about the budget, about such and such a bill, about
certain amendments to certain bills, introduced by
the Cadets, etc." To this question Lenin replied,
in a burst of laughter: "My dear man, what do
you want a budget, an amendment, a bill for? You
are workmen and the Duma exists for the ruling
classes. You simply step forward and tell all
Russia in simple language about the life and toil of
the working class. Describe the horrors of capitalist rule, summon the workers to make a revolution, and fling into the face of this reactionary Duma
that its members are scoundrels and exploiters.
You had better introduce a 'bill' stating that in
three years' time we shall take you all, landlords and
capitalists, and hang you on the lamp-posts. That
would be a real bill!"

The conquest of power, not the execution of
a carefully detailed program of communism,
that was the first and essential element in the
theory and practice of the Bolsheviki. Accordingly they made use of the concrete historic

forces at work in the summer and autumn of 1917 for the purpose of raising themselves to power. The first of those forces was the wide-spread and growing passion for peace among the Russian masses. It is not necessary to recapitulate here the sufferings, losses, and agonies out of which the bitter cry for peace sprang. There was the fact. It appeared among the soldiers at the front and the peasants at home. And it will be remembered that the army was composed mainly of peasants.

By following the course of events from the overthrow of the Tsar's government in March, 1917, to the triumph of the Bolsheviki in November, one can see how insistent was the popular demand for an end to the war. The new Provisional Government had hardly got under way before it was compelled to bow before the storm. On March 27 the Petrograd soviet issued its historic address denouncing the war as an imperialist enterprise and demanding an immediate peace on the basis of no annexations, no indemnities, and the right of self-determination. So great was the popular pressure behind this manifesto that the Provisional Government was compelled to give heed. It was even forced to announce this as the official program of Russia and to transmit it to the allies. In carrying out this promise, however, the Foreign Minister, Miliukov, added a communication of his own which in effect repudiated the peace program. As Miliukov conscientiously believed in the annexationist policies of the former imperial government, he could hardly have done otherwise; but the effect of his virtual repudiation of the soviet program was an uprising in Petrograd which brought about his resignation from office.

Still underestimating the revolutionary force of the peace party, the Provisional Government, on the insistence of the Allies, undertook the fateful offensive of July 1, which ended in the rout of the Russian army. This was followed by another uprising in Petrograd, an uprising under Bolshevik influence if not under that leadership. The revolt was put down and the Bolshevik chiefs were either imprisoned or exiled. Peace agitation continued unabated. The advocates of war thereupon decided that the Provisional Government was too weak for the occasion. Choosing as their agent, Kornilov, the commander-in-chief, they attempted an uprising of their own. This stroke which failed utterly, owing to the want of popular support, merely strengthened the hands of those bent on peace at all costs, and naturally their avowed friends, the Bolsheviki.

The latter made the most of the opportunity. In their attempt to conquer power, they summoned to their side all those who wished to stop the war at once. And the peasants and soldiers answered them. After their day of triumph, the Bolsheviki adopted, as their first article of faith, peace among the warring nations. The Soviet Government issued an official invitation to all the belligerents to suspend hostilities, conclude an armistice, and make a peace on the basis of no annexations and no indemnities. Failing to secure a favorable response from the

Allied governments, the Bolsheviki assumed full responsibility for taking Russia out of the war. They
concluded the treaty of Brest-Litovsk with Germany
and Austria. Those Russians who wanted peace
with the Central Powers got it. They had the
Bolsheviki to thank for it. Thus Lenin and Trotzky made use of one of the great historic forces
that was sweeping through Russia in the summer
and autumn of 1917—the passion for peace.

The second great historic force with which those
who hoped to govern Russia had to reckon was the
passion of the peasants for the land. We are
not now concerned with the origin and development
of that movement. The Russian peasants had been
emancipated in 1861, but the terms of emanicpation
imposed heavy burdens upon them. Russia in 1917
was still a country of great estates. The peasants
struggled under a load of rents and taxes that had
grown heavier with the passing years. Many an
angry uprising had borne witness to the intensity
of their desperation. In the old régime, the peasants saw only slavery. There was promise in the
new Provisional Government, but the spring and
summer of 1917 passed without bringing to the
peasants their coveted land. The Provisional Government, controlled as it was mainly by bourgeois
and liberals, had neither the hot desire nor relentless
will needed for the revolutionary stroke of destroying landlordism absolutely and without compensation. This required the same kind of reckless and
indomitable will that had made peace at all costs.

Nevertheless it was patent to all thoughtful Russians that some solution of the land question could not be avoided without peril to the existing order. The Bolsheviki knew well enough that the peasants were historically no friends of communism. Yet they were bent on the conquest of power and the peasant movement was a living, driving force that offered to sweep them on to success. For this we have the words of Trotzky himself. "The war has assigned a decisive rôle in the events of the revolution to the army. The old army meant the peasantry. Had the revolution developed more normally—that is, under peaceful circumstances as it had in 1912—the proletariat would always have held a dominant position while the peasant masses would gradually have been taken in tow by the proletariat and drawn into the whirlpool of the revolution. But the war produced an altogether different succession of events. The army welded the peasants together, not by a political but by a military tie."

Is it not significant that at the very first session of the council of the soviets after the November revolution, Lenin introduced and carried two decrees —one of them for peace and the second on the land question? Number two on the Bolshevik program was the decree nationalizing all the land held by the imperial family, the church, and the great landlords. The small peasants and the Cossacks were exempted from the operation of the law. All the land so nationalized was transferred, to use the Bolshevist euphemism, "to the peasantry at large."

Thus the second great historic force of which the Bolshevists made use was no more inherently communistic than the first. On the contrary, it was in spirit and form diametrically opposed to all communistic devices. It was founded on deep-seated individualism and it nourished the spirit of egoism. No one knew this better than the socialists. A thousand pamphlets and treatises attest this fact. Surely no Bolshevik leaders were deceived by the phrase "transferred to the peasantry at large." If any of them was so innocent as to suppose that it meant anything more than peasant proprietorship in practice, he was certainly undeceived before the lapse of many months.

Third and last upon the immediate program of the Bolsheviki was a decree appealing directly to labor. It instituted a system of shop control by labor committees. According to the Bolshevik formula it was intended to establish "a control of production by working class committees supervising all the industrial establishments of their respective localities in conjunction with the local soviets and under the control of the Supreme Economic Council, formed by representatives from various people's commissions. This latter was a measure for combatting war-profiteering, speculation, conspiracies of manufacturers against the revolution and other capitalist practices as well as a first step towards the taking over of all means of production by the people." Though avowedly a step in the direction of socialism, it did not, either on its face or in intent, propose an immediate communistic solution of the industrial problem. It did not attempt to destroy the general framework of capitalist society. The position of the existing owners, the compensation of technicians, and the methods of exchange were still unsolved problems. Banks, securities, foreign loans, and the general scheme of capitalist finance still stood. The system was in mortal peril, no doubt. The revolutionary government had announced its ultimate doom, but in November, 1917, many roads to doom were theoretically open. It was not until three months later, namely, February 10, 1918, that the foreign and domestic debt was repudiated, and even then with conditions. It was not until April 23, 1918, that shipping, private banks, and foreign trade were completely nationalized. By May 15, 1918, only about two hundred and thirty industrial enterprises had been nationalized—"half of them for resistance and sabotage."

How the communists would have dealt with the capitalistic structure and processes of the old society if they had enjoyed an opportunity to work out their fate in peace is a matter of pure conjecture. Having ridden into power on a storm of passion and distress, they found themselves, after the morning of victory, still tossed about on a sea of uncertainty. They had yet to reckon with historic forces not of their own choosing. The managers of factories, technicians, telephone operators, government clerks, bank officers, and the rest of the bourgeoisie "sabotaged" the Bolsheviki; gave them an abundance of their own medicine. Kerensky attempted a counter revolution. Kolchak, Denikin,

Yudenitch, and Wrangel raised civil wars against them. British, Japanese, and American forces penetrated Siberia while British and American forces landed at Archangel. The governments of France, England, and the United States in effect, whatever the theory, waged war on Russia. They blockaded Russia. They gave aid and comfort to the enemies of the Bolshevik government. Thus the leaders who had been carried into power by historic forces, not by the appeal of a carefully laid program, found themselves compelled to take up arms against a host of enemies, domestic and foreign. War was the outstanding fact that confronted them on the day after their nominal triumph. Now war is a fact, not a theory. It calls for men, supplies, and movement. Prolonged, sustained, high-tension action springs from deep, unshakable passion. In a period when action is the dominant note, the most passionate, the most radical come to the front. That is what happened in Russia.

It was in the midst of such circumstances that the extreme communist decrees, one after the other, were issued by the Soviet Government. The facts of chronology are not to be disputed. That the Bolsheviki had preached class hatred and extreme measures in and out of season for years is not to be questioned. That fact stands. That they had advocated social or common ownership of the means of production is likewise a fact. But it was not their program that carried them into power. It was their unrelenting will to make peace and give land to the peasants that drew to them a force sufficient for the conquest of the state. Had they been permitted to work out their program without interruption by foreign and domestic wars it is impossible to say just what processes they would have followed. Anyway that is a matter of idle speculation. The truth is that they had to move forward day by day in the midst of powerful and well-nigh baffling forces. Their conduct during the revolution and immediately afterward shows them to be opportunists in matters of politics and economics. They did not attempt to apply at one blow the entire communist program. They delayed and temporized within the limits of the maintenance of their dominion. Their extreme measures, as chronology shows, were born in the midst of extreme dangers and difficulties. That these measures would have come anyway may be argued by all and sundry, but the discussion of such a theorem is a sheer waste of time.

Long afterward, when the many failures of their communist policy were only too evident, the Bolshevik leaders declared that they had been forced into their Utopian devices by events beyond their own control. In a speech delivered in October, 1921, Lenin took this position. "If one recalls our previous economic literature and what our communists were writing before our assumption of power . . . ," he said, "one will see that in this period, when we had not finished the first task of building up the soviet power and had only just emerged from the imperialist war, we talked of our tasks of economic reconstruction much more guardedly and circumspectly than during the second half of 1918 and during the whole of 1919 and 1920. One may refer, for instance, to such decisions as the decree of the All-Russian Central Executive Committee of April 29, 1918 which pointed out the necessity of reckoning with village economy, dealt with the rôle of state capitalism in the construction of socialism, and laid stress upon the significance of one-man responsibility in civil administration as distinct from the tasks connected with political and military power. . . . Partly under the influence of the military tasks with which we were suddenly overwhelmed and partly owing to the desperate position, as it seemed, of the Republic, we made the mistake of trying to bring about an immediate transition to communist production and distribution. . . . A brief experience served to convince us that this was a mistake and contrary to what we had formerly written on the transition from capitalism to socialism, and that if we did not pass through the period of socialist accounting and control it would be impossible to pass even to the lowest stages of communism."

If it be said that Lenin is here indulging himself in a happy after-thought in defence of his reversion to a semi-capitalist system, still it must be conceded on his behalf that he never was deceived by the childish phantasy that paper decrees would establish the new heaven and the new earth. In his famous speech on "The Soviets at Work," delivered in the spring of 1918, he had warned his fellow-communists that they then confronted the real problem of the revolution, namely, that of management, administration, production. "This," he said, "is the most difficult problem. It means the organization of the economic foundations of life for millions of people on a new basis. And it is the most promising problem, for only after its solution shall we be able to say that Russia has become not only a soviet, but a socialist republic."

Again in the course of the same address, he expressed his firm conviction that "the possibility of socialism will be determined by our success in combining soviet rule and the soviet organization of management with the latest progressive measures of capitalism." This is not the doctrine of the fanatic who believes that his system can be applied and will be maintained though the heavens fall. It is the doctrine of the pragmatist who asks of a system: "Will it work?" It shows that even the communist may learn by experience.

Again recognizing the difficulties of prophecy in this rapidly changing world, it appears fairly safe to guess that, in the absence of another violent overturn in Russia, two great economic results will flow from the revolution. Russia will become a huge peasant democracy assimilated in type to the democracies of Rumania, Bulgaria, and Jugoslavia. That much appears certain. A restoration of semi-feudal tenures seems out of the question. If the Bolsheviki continue to hold the reins of power, namely the government and the army, with the support of the peasantry, a form of state capitalism will take the place of communism. Petty industries will flourish under private initiative and the large industries, railways, and natural resources will be exploited by concessionnaires under state supervision. A new middle class may thus be created to dispute the sovereignty of the Bolsheviki. Such a turn in events would of course admit of renewed economic intercourse with the capitalistic nations of the world. But all this may prove to be mere speculation.

Whatever course the domestic economy of Russia may take in the future, however deep may be the influence of the Bolshevik revolution on the internal affairs of Russia, one of the most striking things about it all, at least so far as the United States is concerned, is the new direction given by the Russian cataclysm to the diplomacy and international policies of Europe. It is now conceded that the old Imperialist Russia was one of the most disturbing forces of the modern age. We know from the secret documents recently made public that Russia was a restless, aggressive agent in the organization of forces in the Balkans which precipitated the Great War. Russia was active in stirring France and England to take sides in her behalf. Hating democracy and finding both glory and profit in imperial and military adventures, the Russian oligarchy was one of the most dangerous elements in the world. Its return to power would be a disaster so great that the mind of man could hardly encompass it. The profits that American business men might make from trade with such a system of "law and order" would be a mere bagatelle as compared with the costs of future wars likely to be let loose by Russian imperial policies of the old type.

Even more important than the European complications created by a revival of the old order in Russia would be the disturbance reintroduced into the affairs of the Far East by an imperialist restoration. We now know from the secret papers and treaties taken from Russian archives that the Tsar's government was a relentless foe of the American policy of "the open door." When the revolution broke in Petrograd, the imperialist party was actually arranging to settle scores with the United States in the matter of China. Had the Russian government emerged from the world war intact and with enhanced prestige, no one can doubt, after reading the secret archives now available, that Russia would have taken the lead in the formation of a combination to oust the United States from the Far East. It seems hardly necessary to point out the import of a conjuncture so fraught with danger for this nation.

A less ponderable result of the Russian revolution in the sphere of international relations has been the merciless exposure of the methods, tactics, and designs of secret diplomacy as pursued by all the great powers of Europe without a single exception. By tearing open the archives of Petrograd and publishing the Secret Treaties and the secret correspondence relating to the events that led up to the Great War, the Bolsheviki gave a shock to the solid structure of diplomatic intrigue and chicanery from which it will hardly recover. The full effect of this exposure has not yet been felt. In the course of the next ten or twenty years it will have reached the mind of the vast masses of mankind. It is doubtful whether any government will then be able to pursue the discredited methods with the same reckless disregard for consequences. The old diplomacy will by no means disappear, but the sword of Damocles will hang over the head of the government which practices methods that have wrought such wreckage in Europe. Another concussion such as that which shook the world from 1914 to 1918, arising from the same imperialist intrigues and deceptions, would doubtless produce new revolutions that would stagger the imagination. By the exposure of secret diplomacy, the Bolsheviki contributed immeasurably to enlightening mankind on the methods and devices so perilous to peace and human welfare. Whatever their motives, the result has been tremendous. When the slow moving but terrific forces of public opinion set in train by this action come to bear with full force on the governments of the world a peaceful revolution will be wrought in international relations. This may be the most momentous outcome of the Russian cataclysm. The diplomat of our time may well learn from Butler's lines on Shaftesbury:

> *Our state-artificer foresaw*
> *Which way the world began to draw.*
> *For as old sinners have all the points*
> *O, th' compass in their bones and joints,*

Can by their pains and aches find
All turns and changes of the wind,
And better than by Napier's bones
Feel in their own the age of moons:
So guilty sinners in a state
Can by their crimes prognosticate
And in their consciences feel pain
Some days before a shower of rain.

VII

THE RISE OF NEW PEASANT DEMOCRACIES

THOUGH bread remains as of old the very staff of life and must come as of old from the open fields, the thought of the modern world is mainly urban. The cities are the centres of modern discussion. There are to be found the writers, the makers of books and newspapers, the politicians and the statesmen, the clergy, the various organs of opinion and propaganda, the libraries, the parliaments, the cabinets, and the forums for debate and discussion. Since most of the thinkers whose ideas find expression in print are urban, naturally the city is the object of their interest and their speculation. The problems of finance, business, commerce, industry, and labor thus inevitably occupy the foreground of modern thought. For every editorial that touches the widestretching fields of the countryside there are a hundred bearing upon the conflicts of capital and labor, the methods of municipal government and politics, and the foundations of stocks and bonds. For every book on agrarian economy, there are a score on industrial economy, finance, and socialism. The news that crowds the pages of our daily journals, save in a

time of populistic disturbances, is the news of the
city and its industries. Even the plots of the moving pictures, excepting the Wild West shows, are
mostly laid in cities and depict urban rather than
country life. When the farmer and his wife ride
to town in a Ford to see the fleeting film, they do
not look upon Cincinnatus at the plow, but Douglas
Fairbanks climbing a twenty-story office building.
So the mind of the farmer and peasant becomes
submerged in and subdued by the urban mind. To
the natural economic forces driving the rural population into the cities is added the powerful drawing
force of urban thought which, superficially at least,
colors all news, all art, all economic discussion, all
literature, all politics.

And yet though this is true, the country remains
as in the days of Solon and the days of the Gracchi
the basis of all life. Many a melancholy spectacle
demonstrates this axiomatic truth with terrible emphasis. If you will read carefully Fowler's interesting book on Roman Society or Davis' equally
fascinating work on Wealth in Ancient Rome you
will find a marvellous picture of daily life in the
homes, banking houses, and streets of the immortal
city on the banks of the Tiber. In these books you
can learn how a vast urban population was brought
together and sustained, only to be dispersed. You
can see with your mind's eye the great banking
houses along the Appian Way from which bills,
drafts, and orders went out to the ends of the known
world. You can see the markets thronged by the
merchants of every clime dealing in tin and lead from

Britain and silk and spices from the Far East.   The vast structures of business, finance, commerce, industry, like the huge deep-founded arches of the Augustan palace, seemed eternal.   And yet how ephemeral it was after all!   An invading army in a few hours could sack and burn the city, kill or scatter its population, and paralyse its business operations.   Violence and decay restored to the open country—to the fields of Italy—the sceptre that had been wrested from it.   The cities of the ancient world fell into decay, Augustan palaces grovelled in the dust, grass grew in the streets; but life in the open country remained.   There were disturbances, forays, and disorders, of course, after the rule of the Eternal City was broken but even invading barbarians knew that bread was the staff of life.   So it happened that the people of Italy today—those that pursue their callings now on the banks of the Tiber or labor with the vine and olive under the endless cloud that steams from Vesuvius—are descendants, not of the orators and merchants of Cicero's day, but of the men and women who tilled the soil of Italy while politicians tickled the multitude and the merchants chaffered in their counting houses.   Again, in our own time, we see the great city of Petrograd sink down in desolation and people fleeing from it into the country as from a plague, because it offers only misery and starvation.   With the causes we are not now concerned, but with the fact—the fundamental fact that every city in the world might be levelled to the dust and countless millions could still live on the earth in a fair degree of comfort and with a good deal more security than the masses of our cities today. On the other hand, let destruction spread over the countryside and every city would sink down in hopeless decay. Its buildings and its counting houses, its tenements and its factories would be the tombs of its inhabitants. This is a commonplace too often forgotten by those who have occasion to write and speak in these days.

If mankind is to endure, the country must endure and while it endures it will exert a deep influence on the economy and policies of nations in the long run in spite of our superficially urban thought. When once the city state was ruled by the crowds that gathered in the open forum, the opinion of the countryside perhaps did not matter so much. Aristotle thought that an agrarian democracy was after all far better and safer than an urban democracy. It was not subject to the influences of crowd psychology, nor was it the source of so many turbulent disputes and conflicts. The Greek philosopher, therefore, flatly declared that " the best material for a democracy is an agricultural population. . . . Being poor, they have no leisure and therefore do not often attend the assembly and not having the necessaries of life they are always at work and do not covet the property of others."

From Aristotle's day to our own, the agricultural population has figured in the thought and policy of the most far-sighted statesmen. It is sometimes assumed that Aristotle's dictum about the soil-tilling people is of general application in all times and all places. Again and again in political literature there appears the notion that an agricultural population is essentially conservative—a secure and stable foundation for a state. Such was the view of Thomas Jefferson. Even Daniel Webster, far more urban in his thinking, looked upon landed property widely distributed as the best guarantee for republican institutions.

"Widely distributed." There is the rub. A contented peasantry, not too heavily burdened with taxation, allowed to pursue its course in peace is usually a stable and orderly population. But all peasants in all times have not been contented. History affords numerous examples of terrible uprisings led by tillers of the soil. The Peasants' Revolt in England in the year 1383 was a historic outbreak from the countryside. Again in Martin Luther's day the peasants in many parts of Germany rose against their lords and wrought havoc far and wide, calling down upon their heads the stern wrath of the Wartburg reformer. Long afterward the peasants of France laid their urgent grievances before the king and ruling classes, and in the stirring days of the great revolution made known their passion for the soil by raiding and burning the châteaux of their lords and masters. As a result of their uprisings, about one half of the land of France passed into peasant proprietorship. The direct exploitation of the tillers of the soil on a large scale disappeared over half the superficial area of land. Then an era of contentment set in. The peasants, once the source and support of revolutionary fervor, became the stabilizers of society—the one element that could be counted upon to rally to the support of government in any contest with the proletariat. Having got their portion of the earth's goods by revolution, they were for propriety and property and public order.

In central and eastern Europe, however, the ideas of the French agrarian revolution were slow in coming into force. It is true that in western and southern Germany serfdom was on the wane in 1789 and a free tenantry was taking the place of bondmen. It is true also that the famous agrarian reforms of Stein and Hardenberg begun in 1807 transformed the feudal régime of old Prussia. Long afterward by many decrees and laws the peasants of eastern Europe were freed from the more irksome and degrading badges of servitude. This for example is what happened in 1861 when the Tsar of Russia by a sweeping imperial edict declared the old bondage at an end. When the Great War broke upon the world in 1914, the servile incidents of feudalism as a legal system had disappeared in even the most remote parts of eastern Europe.

But we should not mistake the sign for the substance. In point of fact, while the peasants of Russia were nominally free after 1861, they were burdened by heavy economic obligations. They had to pay dearly for their supposed freedom. The Russian government undertook to compensate the landlords for their lost rights and in turn the government set about the odious task of collecting from the peasants. It so happened therefore that the state was a more terrible master than the old landlord.

Often the latter was tender-hearted and in times of
distress could be moved by pleas of poverty, but
the officers of the state were inexorable. So the
peasant of Russia found his cup of freedom filled
with bitter dregs. Moreover vast estates owned by
landlords and by the imperial family were not dissolved by the act of emancipation. The peasant
proprietors were loaded with taxes and idemnities
and wide reaches of arable land were tilled by ten-
ants and laborers. Here were the seeds of that
revolutionary zeal that flamed up again and again
in the Tsar's realm with such ghastly effects—revolutions and reprisals which for sheer horror deserve
comparison with the servile revolts and crucifixions
of ancient times.

In East Prussia, Hungary, and Rumania, as
in Russia, the system of great estates remained undisturbed by the emancipation of the serfs. East
Prussia was the home of the Prussian Junker, the
bulwark of the Hohenzollern family, professional
militarism, and autocratic pretensions. In Hungary
and Rumania the position of the peasantry was even
worse than in Prussia where at least some efforts
were made to lift the tiller of the soil by education.
An enlightened English traveller says of Hungary
in 1914: "Hungary was a mediaeval state var-
nished over with an appearance of modernity. Real
power was in the hands of the great nobles and
the smaller landowners, and the great landlord
ruled on his estate with almost unfettered authority,
having his own court of justice where his own peasants would be tried and condemned for acts offen-

sive to his rule. It was customary to consider and treat the peasant as an inferior species of creature with whom the only arguments which would avail were blows. . . . The privileged classes had all the dress, manners, and appearance of civilized Western Europeans, but on their estates feudal homage was paid to them, their peasants were kicked and flogged like—peasants." In Rumania, still further east, the state of the peasant was perhaps worse, if anything, than in Hungary. A terrible revolt in 1907 bore witness to the fierce discontent of the laborers on the land. The single, eloquent fact that eleven thousand of them were killed before "order could be restored" revealed both the desperation of the peasant and the tenacity of landlordism.

Without taking time to go into greater details as to the surviving areas of servitude, we may conclude with the general statement that in 1914 millions of Russians, Poles, Prussians, Hungarians, and Rumanians lived on the land in a state of economic bondage—far removed from that of the free peasant proprietor of France or the Rhine country. Whoever, in his urban-mindedness overlooks that vital, basic fact, overlooks a matter of transcendent importance in the economic and political life of the modern world.

Of all the revolutions wrought by the cataclysm of the Great War none was more fraught with significance for the multitude than the agrarian revolution in Russia which was the forerunner of other revolutions, less drastic but leading finally to similar results in wide sections of eastern Europe. All accounts of the Russian revolution of November, 1917, those that condemn as well as those that praise, show the revolutionary zeal of the peasant soldiers fused with that of the workingmen of the cities. Had the provisional government set up under Kerensky dared to take the harsh and revolutionary step of destroying landlordism without compensation at one blow, it seems that the later Bolshevist uprising would have been without the support necessary to success. Be that as it may, all agree that the peasants furnished a strong support for the November or Bolshevik revolution of 1917. According to Trotzky, the avowed champion of the proletariat, "the war assigned a decisive rôle in the events of the revolution to the army. The army meant the peasants."

Why did the Russian peasant differ from the French peasant in 1917 and furnish the materials for a radical social revolution? Was it because he understood the abstruse theories of Karl Marx better than did Jacques Bonhomme? Was it because the eloquence of Trotzky excelled the eloquence of Marcel Cachin? Not at all. The Russian peasant, like the French peasant of August 4, 1789, wanted the land to till and was ready to resort to violence to get it. By 1917 however the working classes of the Russian cities had grown in numbers, in organization, in power, and in solidarity so that it was with the proletariat rather than the bourgeois that the Russian peasant united in attaining his ends. The driving force of the land-lust is shown, as we have seen above, in the early decrees of the Bolshevik government. First was peace. The second was land for the peasants. The third was workers' control in the factories—not socialism or even communism as yet.

After peace, the land. Therein lies the secret of the Bolshevik revolution. The Marats and Robespierres of Petrograd were daring enough to give soil to the peasants without indemnities to the expropriated. After peace, the very first domestic measure of the Bolsheviki was the ousting of the landlords. To use again the language of a Bolshevik, Litvinov, this momentous decree "transferred to the peasantry at large all lands hitherto in possession of private landlords, of the imperial family, of the church, etc., to be administered and distributed for use by peasant committees acting in conjunction with the local soviets, on such a basis that no one should receive more land than he and his family could cultivate efficiently without hired labor or less land than is required for his own and his family's needs." The fundamental law of socialization which went into effect in September, 1918, did but elaborate this general principle. It is true that in juridical theory the ownership of the land "passes over to the use of the entire laboring population without any compensation, open or secret, to the former owners," but in practice the peasant who tills the soil possesses it in spite of parchment, seals, and decrees. Thus by one of the ironies of history, a vast free peasantry, the bulwark of conservatism, will be created by the orders of the world's extreme radicals. The irony may pass. The fact remains.

While the revolutionary crisis was engineered in Germany by the spokesmen of the working class as in Russia it was not supported to the same extent by the peasantry. As we have seen the system of great estates did not prevail extensively outside of Prussia. The peasants of Saxony and Bavaria, for example, were as contented as any agricultural population in the world. A close examination of the records shows moreover that the German revolution of 1918 was due to a breakdown of the old ruling class rather than an impassioned uprising of the masses in town and country. Nevertheless, the German revolutionists looked upon the great estates of Prussia with feelings akin to those entertained by the Bolsheviki. The left wing of the Socialist party advocated immediate and unconditional nationalization of those estates, but its views were rejected by the Majority Socialists. The latter, afraid to lay hold of the great industries, showed even more hesitation when confronted with a proposition to apply socialization to the land.

Nevertheless, with the aid of the bourgeois, especially of the liberal persuasion, and with the aid of the Center or Catholic party which entertained no love for the Protestant Junkertum of Prussia, the Socialists, under whose auspices the direction of affairs fell, at least made an attack on the land problem. The national convention embodied in the new constitution of 1919 a general clause relative to the land. "The distribution and use of the land are supervised by the state in such a way as to pre-

vent its misuse and promote the object of ensuring
to every German a healthful dwelling and to all
German families, especially those with numerous
children, homesteads corresponding to their needs.
War veterans shall receive special consideration in
the enactment of a homestead law.   Landed property the acquisition of which is necessary to satisfy
the demand for housing, to promote settlement and
reclamation or to improve agriculture may be expropriated.   Entailments shall be dissolved.   The
cultivation and utilization of the soil is a duty of
the landowner towards the community.   An increase in the value of land arising without the application of labor or capital to the property shall
inure to the benefit of the community as a whole.
All mineral resources and all economically useful
forces of nature are subject to the control of the
state." Such are the terms of Article 155 of the
Weimar Constitution of 1919.

The general language of the fundamental law of
the land was supplemented by decrees and legislation.   In July of 1919, even before the national
assembly had concluded its work, the federal government issued a decree on small gardens and small
farms providing for the rental or lease of lands not
used profitably by the present owners.   By a federal
law of the same year an obligation was laid upon
the German states to undertake land settlements and
to encourage the creation of small farms.   Provision
was made for transferring state lands to settlement
associations and for conferring upon them the right
of preëmption in the sale of tracts of land of less

than twenty-five hectares. The law went further.
It stipulated that in those districts in which more
than ten per cent of the arable land is in the hands
of large holders possessing more than one hundred
hectares each, associations of landlords for the disposal of lands must be formed. Such associations
were required to turn over to settlement associations,
on the basis of fair compensation, a certain proportion of their estates. The government of Prussia,
following the injunction thus issued, served notice on
the great landlords that compulsory expropriation
would follow if they did not voluntarily cut up and
sell their estates. The ultimate effect of these legal
provisions remains to be seen. The revolution in
Germany was not so thoroughgoing as in Russia.

Still it is not to be doubted that the appetite of
the peasants for the land was whetted. The old
order with the old spirit will be difficult to restore.

Between Prussia and Russia lies Poland, long the
paradise of great landlords. Swept by war and
wracked by revolution, the agricultural system of
that unhappy land was shaken to the foundation,
but the feudal estate survived the storm in many
sections and the Polish aristocracy received no such
blow as that dealt to the nobility of Russia. The
revolutionary feeling in town and country, however,
made untenable the old position of the landlords.
Under strong and insistent radical pressure two significant land laws were enacted by the Polish Diet,
the first in 1919 and the second during the following
year. The opening sections of the latter law reveal
the spirit of the new order: "The agricultural pol-

icy of the Polish republic should be based, above all, on good, well-organized peasants' farms of different types and acreage, capable of intensive cultivation and based on private ownership. . . . The owners of the land may only be persons who will work themselves, or their heirs, with the exception of that land which will be placed at the disposal of the landless proprietor and which is exploited by municipal or rural bodies." The technical provisions of the legislation carrying these principles into effect need not detain us here. We may conclude with the observation of a student well-versed in Polish affairs, Dr. Guest, that "land reform in Poland will certainly go on because there is no way of resisting it except by sheer reaction and as the peasants have the support of the socialist town workers, the two wings of democracy are united." Still this is prophecy.

To the southwest of Poland the new republic of Czechoslovakia was carried into the current of land reform by revolutionary fervor. With a socialistic President and a parliament composed in large part of socialist and radical members, it was inevitable that the feudal régime should be attacked. Within a few weeks after the wreck of Austria in November, 1918, the Czechs had undertaken many fundamental changes in the old régime. All titles of nobility, orders, and distinctions were swept away in one decree. Another, adopted before the declaration of independence was two weeks old, provided for the division of the great estates. The domains held by the former reigning families, by

enemies of the state, and by offenders against the
republic were confiscated without compensation.
The technical details of land distribution were set
forth at length in a great land law enacted on January 30, 1920, based upon the broad principle that
"the land shall be given in the first place to those
able to cultivate it." The execution of the law was
vested in local commissions representing the various
political groups, with a view to assuring the effective enforcement of its terms. While this had an
unfortunate effect upon scientific administration, it
seemed to give a guarantee that the redistribution of
the land would be thoroughgoing. Czechoslovakia
is destined to have its rich and diversified industries complemented by a large landowning peasantry.
Already it seems to offer more promise of stability
than any of the new creations of central and eastern
Europe.

How different was the fortune of Czechoslovakia's
former partner in the Hapsburg empire, Hungary.
One of the most conservative and mediaeval countries of Europe in 1914, it fell for a short time into
the hands of Bolshevik extremists after the revolution of 1918. Though the communist régime was
soon liquidated and a White Terror inaugurated, the
great landlords did not quite recover their former
power or their serene indifference to the peasant
movement. On the contrary, frightened within an
inch of their lives by their experience with the dictatorship of the proletariat and by the course of
events in Russia, they decided to fight fire with fire.
By a law enacted in 1920, they provided in rather

generous terms for a division of estates and a peasant proprietorship. As the law was not self-enforcing and the government was in the hands of landlords the future of the promised agrarian revolution seemed in doubt. However, a trained English observer who has recently journeyed through Hungary says: "Universal suffrage gained by the revolution plus a peasant proprietor program, forced by fear of Bolshevism, has made the peasants into a very strong power and much stronger than the landowners bargained for. Some of the best observers in Hungary think that politics for years to come will group around the fight between big landowners and the peasants over the land. All other politics will depend on that. The question of the return of the Hapsburgs is only a move in this contest for, to the big landlords, the Hapsburg family represents the old régime, as it does to the military class who support the policy of return, because without it, their own orders and distinctions no longer have the same value and importance. Anti-Semitism is only a move in this contest, easily to be explained when one learns that the Church is one of the greatest landlords in Hungary and one of the most wordly."

Like Hungary, the neighboring state of Rumania passed through the dissolving and liquidating process of defeat and revolution. It had long been the home of an overbearing ruling class and an oppressed peasantry, perhaps the most benighted in Europe outside of Russia. The fires of the peasant revolt that had broken out in 1907 were still smoldering when the Rumanian armies were defeated and the

Germans took possession of the capital. Then the old régime became bankrupt and Rumania was suddenly transformed into the semblance of a peasant democracy. Sweeping decrees established universal manhood suffrage and ordered the redistribution of the land, nearly half of which was concentrated in the hands of about 4000 landlords. The Bolshevik revolution in Bessarabia facilitated the process; when that province was later annexed a new revolutionary virus was added to that already existing in Rumania. The ferment grew from day to day. The Rumanian parliament, subject to irresistible pressure, then made the first land law still more radical by adopting many of the extreme provisions of the Bessarabian settlement. According to the latest reports, the 4000 landlords were vigorously fighting for liberal compensation with small prospect of collecting it. The landlords were dethroned and the process of distribution was taking place in a crude fashion under the eyes of the village mayors and schoolmasters. Reaction is on the horizon, no doubt, but the old order of 1914 is shaken to its foundations.

Thoroughgoing as was the revolution in Rumania, it can hardly be compared with the sweeping character of that in Bulgaria. When the Bulgarian government went into bankruptcy with the exhaustion of the Central Powers, the whole governing class was shattered. Those who had conspired to bring the war about and had profiteered during the struggle were tried and imprisoned. The vigorous leader of the opposition to war, the spokesman of the peasants, Stamboulisky, who had been imprisoned for his activities and views, was released and made prime minister of his stricken country. Bulgaria became a peasant nation. Its government, its cabinet, and its chief minister were peasants. Next in number in the parliament were the communists and socialists, while the bourgeois could hardly muster enough to make any impression on the course of politics.

The leaders of the Bulgarian peasants have launched a "Green Communism" and issued a ringing call to the tillers of the soil everywhere to form a "Green International." With swinging periods that sound like the Communist Manifesto, the Bulgarians call upon the peasants of all lands to unite and enter upon their inheritance. "Across the vista of human progress there runs like a white thread," opens the Green Manifesto, " the history of a class which has everywhere and always been compelled to submit to unjust and evil treatment." It closes: "The international union of the peasant masses of all lands will be founded, and the voice of the peasant too long silent will be heard. This union is the great event of the new era and the importance of an understanding and close relation among the peasants will have a vast significance in the international affairs of the future. We wait for this with joyful heart and cherish the hope that the Union will improve the hard lot of the peasants of the world." A military dictatorship is the only alternative to peasant government in Bulgaria.

Across the border in Jugoslavia, the ferment is at work. Already a land of peasant proprietors, it is being stirred by the new currents of thought that run fast among the long silent tillers of the soil. In the convention which drafted the constitution of 1921, the radicals, communists, and agrarians were in an overwhelming majority. The fundamental law framed by them strikes a blow at landlordism of the old type. The feudal relationships existing on the estates in the regions wrested from Austria-Hungary are dissolved and the vassals on those estates are given their lands without compensation to the former owners. It is decreed that the expropriation of the great estates and their division into properties for the benefit of tillers of the land shall be effected by law. No compensation is to be granted to former reigning families and to those who received their land from foreign authorities. Entails are abolished. The large forests are nationalized and state aid is to be given to producers on the land. The Serbs, Croats, and Slovenes, therefore, are moving rapidly toward a democracy of the peasant type, thus lending their powerful encouragement to the vast mass of tillers of the soil who occupy a broad belt of land stretching from the Adriatic to the Baltic.

Can it be doubted that the events just recited will have a far-reaching influence on the course of politics in Eastern Europe during the years to come? Prophecy is not the business of the historian, but one cannot help comparing these events with the momentous record of the French revolution. While the economist may inquire whether the system of peasant proprietorship is as productive as enlightened landlordism, the inquiry seems academic. If a contented peasantry can be established, will it not work in the long run for stability and peace? Indeed, can there be social peace without it? At all events here is a power with which statesmen must reckon as surely as they must reckon with organized labor and combined capital.

VIII

SOCIALISM AND THE LABOR
MOVEMENT

THE influence of the war upon socialist thought and activity was so deep and so far-reaching that no single phrase may be safely employed to describe it. Undoubtedly division, dissension, and disillusionment were among the outstanding characteristics. But these do not exhaust the subject. During the war all the belligerent governments employed the principles of state socialism on a large scale to obtain the national cohesion and degree of production necessary for carrying on the conflict. In laying taxes, parliaments made distinctions among the various kinds of incomes, which only served to emphasize one of the cardinal points in the socialist indictment of the capitalistic order. Organized labor secured a weight in the councils of nations and in the conduct of affairs so great that even the fate of cabinets depended upon its decisions. While labor relaxed its rules and restrictions in the management of industry it developed ideas and practices of factory control that were new in the history of economy. Trade unionists of the old type, accustomed to consider only hours and wages and equally accustomed to carrying on war against socialistic doctrines, found themselves compelled by the stress of circumstances to accept the idea of compulsory labor and to coöperate more and more with socialist leaders. The German government, long the open foe of the Social Democrats, was forced with the passing months of war to rely more and more upon their support and in the end, it seems, escaped a domestic revolution by relinquishing all authority into their hands. Since the war, naturally, the tide has receded but the old landmarks do not bear just the same aspect.

On the subject of disillusionment, though it is subtle in its essence, much can be said. The first great dream to be dispelled was the power of the socialists to prevent war. The feeble attempt of the German and French socialists to come to common terms in the fateful August days of 1914 was a complete failure. The French socialists supported their government because, they said, the war was one of defence against Imperialist Germany and their government had kept them informed of the course of events. The German Social Democrats gave a support equally loyal to their government on the ground that the war was one of defence against Imperialist Russia, although they could not say with truth that they had enjoyed the confidence of the Chancellor or his colleagues during the rhetorical flourishes that preceded it. Minorities dissented and fought to the bitter end, paying the full penalty for their temerity, but official socialism proved no barrier to the war passions that swept Europe into the maelstrom and held it there for four long, bitter years.

It may be urged, of course, that no one familiar with the numerical strength of the socialists and with their pre-war policies expected them to muster the power necessary to stop war. Indeed this is often urged. Statesmen, it is said, had correctly estimated this force in making their calculations. But we have high authority for the proposition that some astute socialists counted on no such outcome. We are told by Zinoviev, in his brief life of Lenin, that neither of them expected the complete breakdown of the German Social Democrats. These two men were together in Galicia when the war broke out. As soon as the news reached them Zinoviev said to his friend: "You will see, the German Democrats will not dare to vote against the war, but will abstain in the vote on war credits." To this Lenin replied: "No, they are not such scoundrels after all. They will not, of course, fight the war, but they will, to ease their conscience, vote against the credits in order that the working class may not rise against them." Zinoviev then goes on with the story: "In this case Lenin was wrong and so was I. Neither of us had taken the full measure of the flunkeyism of the Social Patriots. The European Social Democrats proved complete bankrupts. They all voted for war credits. When the first number of *Vorwärts,* the organ of the German Social Democrats, reached us with the news that they had voted the war credits, Lenin at first refused to believe. 'It cannot be,' he said, 'it must be a forged number. Those scoundrels, the German bourgeois, have specially published such a number of the *Vorwärts* in order to compel us to go against the International.' Alas, it was not so." Thus at least two leaders, long associated with international socialism, agitators and students, were disillusioned.

I. SOCIALISTS CONFRONTED BY THE REALITIES OF POWER

It also happened in the economy of things that the two men who thus saw a grand mirage fade before their eyes in August, 1914, were destined themselves to play leading rôles in a drama which lifted socialist hopes to high heaven and dashed them again to earth. In this connection it is not necessary to make use of any statements made by enemies of Soviet Russia. The course of affairs can be traced in the writings of Lenin and his supporters. We may also accept, for the sake of argument, the Bolshevik contention that the counter-revolutionary movements, the wars waged against the Bolshevik government by enemies within as well as without, and the iron blockade imposed by the great powers were mainly responsible for the further deterioration in the ruin left by the old régime. The Russian revolution of November, 1917, opened with confident appeals to the proletariat of the world to follow the example of Petrograd. The hopes of the extremists were raised everywhere. In Italy, Spain, Hungary, and Germany, attempts were made to emulate the Muscovite example. All this stands upon the open record. All these efforts failed. As the months passed Moscow was forced to admit that it had been deceived, that the world was not ripe for a proletarian revolution. Thus one great fiction was dissipated.

Equally significant was the failure of the Bolshevik system as a recuperative and reconstructive force. It did not call forth the productive energies of the Russian people. The task of overturning the provisional government and seizing the power of the state was relatively simple and easy. On the morning of victory came the real test, namely, that of producing and distributing goods. In this, the Bolsheviki confronted new and baffling undertakings for which neither their philosophy nor their technical knowledge fitted them. It has been said that the ruins they inherited were almost beyond repair. That may be granted also for the sake of argument. Still with all the machinery of the state in their hands, the Russian socialists failed to start Russia on the path to recuperation. Hence the necessity of falling back upon capitalism, modified and restrained, if you please, but still capitalism.

For this, too, we have the words of the Russian premier, Lenin. In a speech delivered early in 1921 he laid before his communist colleagues two alternatives. "We can," he said, "completely prohibit and prevent the development of private non-state exchange, that is, commerce, or in other words capitalism, which is inevitable with the existence of millions of small producers. Such a policy would be stupid and suicidal for the party which attempted to carry it out. It would be stupid because it is economically impossible. It would be suicidal because the party that attempted to carry it out would inevitably collapse. It is useless trying to conceal the sin into which some communists 'in thought, in word and in deed,' have fallen with regard to this policy. We shall attempt to rectify this error. It is essential that we rectify this error or else it will go hard with us."

Then Lenin presented the other alternative: "Or (and this is the only possible and sensible policy) we can refrain from prohibiting and preventing the development of capitalism and strive to direct it in the path of state capitalism. This is economically possible, for state capitalism exists in one form or another everywhere that elements of free trade and capitalism in general are to be found."

The implications of this are clear enough. The Bolsheviki conquered the power of the state and found themselves practically helpless in the presence of technical problems of production. It was one thing to seize the factories; it was another thing to manage them and to carry on all the intricate processes of production and distribution. But with all the symbols and trappings of state in their hands they could not find the secret springs from which productive energies flow. They could not, with all their decrees and parchment and sealing wax, prevent the peasant from holding the soil that he tilled. They could not set mills, mines, and factories in the full swing of operation. They laid the cause of their defeat upon the technical and clerical forces that committed sabotage against their orders. That

too may be conceded for the sake of argument.
But the fact remains that the first great communist
state established in the world had to go back to a
modified form of capitalism within the brief period
of four years.

The disillusionment that marked this process was
accompanied by the practical lesson that decrees are
not bread and that phraseology makes no boots.   If
the return was resisted by any considerable body of
communists in Russia, the news of the fact has not
reached the western hemisphere.   As far as the
English were concerned, a visit of the delegates of
the British Labor Party to Petrograd was sufficient
to dissipate any ardent hopes for an immediate
millenium on the Russian principles.   Only a small,
intransigent party in Germany, the Communist
Labor party, clung to the primitive gospel of the
pure word.   It declared solemnly, late in 1921,
that "the Soviet Government of Russia has ceased to
be a Proletarian government by reason of its concessions to the peasants. . . . The Soviet Government, forced by economic circumstances to introduce capitalism into the country, becomes itself the
representative of capitalism."   As for the rest of
the socialist world, the fond hope that the conquest
of power by the proletariat would automatically
bring something like the millenium or at all events
an endurable system of production has vanished.
Little groups of obdurate communists may defy
Moscow, but facts are what they are.   And it is
with facts that the historian has to deal.

II. SOCIALISM AND THE CENTRAL POWERS

Scarcely less disappointing to the socialists of all countries was the failure of the German Democrats to make the most of their power in the days of their revolution. On the 9th of November the authority of the German state in effect passed into the hands of an extra-legal council composed of Social Democrats and Independents. The first revolutionary government was composed entirely of socialists. Nevertheless no steps were taken in the direction of socialization. The proposal that the socialists should proceed to an economic revolution by means of soldiers and workers councils was rejected under Social Democratic pressure. Instead, a national assembly was summoned with the full knowledge that there would not be a socialist majority in such a body. That was not all. Leaders among the Social Democrats, finding themselves in the seats of the mighty, in positions of full responsibility, openly opposed all radical programs for socialization. On November 19, 1918, the *Freiheit* declared that there was no doubt about the possibility of transforming the great industrial monopolies into common property. A few days later Ebert, the socialist chancellor, replied by denouncing the "visionaries" who demanded an immediate socialization of German industries and warned the people against "experiments." The official commission on socialization declared that the "first condition of all eco-

nomic reorganization was the revival of production,"
as if to say that socialization would not lead to such
a revival or was not even necessary to it, as urged
by socialists of the left. This negative position
was defended on many grounds. It was said for
instance that the socialists should not become the receivers for bankrupt capitalism and that the time
was not ripe for the transition.

The truth is that the German socialists, instead
of presenting a compact front to capitalism on the
day of the revolution were hopelessly divided as to
goals and tactics. They had been divided all during the War. Party rules made the vote for military credits on August 4, 1914, appear unanimous on
the record, but it was known that fourteen votes had
been cast against the government in the party
caucus at which the action had been decided upon.
The division thus made manifest increased with
time. In 1916 a separate group known as the
Social Democratic Alliance made its appearance. In
April of the next year, an Independent Social Democratic party was organized. In the meantime there
had grown up a formless and illegal group still
more radical and bearing the name of Spartacus.
The failure of the Social Democrats and the Independents to bring about the long-heralded proletarian revolution in 1918, led to the formation of a
German Communist party modelled on the Russian
lines and advocating Russian methods.

The Communist party was only a little more than
a year old when signs of cleavage began to appear
within its ranks. These became marked in the

spring of 1920 just after the attempt of Kapp and Lüttwitz to restore the monarchy. Seeing that the radicals were likely to play into the hands of the reactionaries, the executive committee of the Communist party issued a statement (March 21, 1920) to the effect that the time was not ripe for a dictatorship of the proletariat and that political action was appropriate for the hour. This incensed a large number of the intransigents, who clung fervently to the Moscow program. The result was the formation of the German Communist Labor party at a Congress held on April 4, 1920. The new organization approached the authorities of the Third International and while not formally admitted was at first treated kindly and granted a consultative vote.

Not convinced that a proletarian dictatorship was yet a forlorn hope in Germany, the extreme communist left wing undertook to overthrow the capitalist system by a general uprising in March, 1921. There was serious fighting in a number of industrial centres, but the revolt was put down. The members of the right wing in the Communist party denounced the attempt as foolish and as the inevitable result of "infantile" tactics. The extremists answered by saying that, although it failed, the uprising marked another battle in the grand world-wide campaign against capitalism.

In this state of affairs, an appeal was made to Moscow, and in a letter of August 14, 1921, Lenin read the German communists a lesson. He advised them to close up their ranks and quit quarrelling.

He urged them not to give so much attention to the new Communist Labor party, not to advertise it, not to attack it. "They are too lacking in sense," he said, "to be taken seriously, whilst it would be wrong policy to be angry with them. . . . The infantile disease of 'Leftism' will pass and will be completely overcome with the growth of the movement." He also informed them that although the March uprising had added to their knowledge, the communist movement in the majority of countries was far from the goal of its endeavors and not prepared for a successful overturn of the established order.

This letter stirred the Communist Labor party to wrath. At its congress held in September, 1921, it accused the Russian Soviet Government of deserting its post and acting as manager for the bourgeois revolution. The congress therefore proposed a Fourth International based on left-wing communism. In its official organ, the Communist Labor party laid down three propositions: (1) The Third International has betrayed the proletariat and has become the instrument of the bourgeois against the proletariat. (2) The Third International betrayed the proletariat by handing over the leadership of the Proletarian International to the Russian state and its leaders. (3) The Soviet government of Russia has ceased to be a proletarian government by reason of its concessions to the peasants. . . . The soviet government forced by economic circumstances to introduce capitalism into the country, becomes itself the representative of capitalism." Proceeding from these fundamental propositions, the German Communist Labor party feels obliged to establish a new international, to "build upwards from below a real soviet international." The strength of the party was reported as being 36,000 in October, 1921. The confidence of its leaders is, however, unshakable. The conquest of the world is still their fixed goal.

So for one reason or another, the German socialists, divided into fiercely contending factions, let the crisis of the revolution pass by without making a concerted, determined effort to bring about the great socialist transformation which they had long promised. The Social Democratic government turned all the forces of state loose upon the extremists who sought to follow the Russian example. By the irony of circumstances, private property was protected by socialist bayonets and communist uprisings were suppressed by socialist troops. It is true that the Social Democrats made a deep impress upon the new constitution drawn up at Weimar, in 1919, but it will not be forgotten that they were driven to the most radical proposals, namely, those creating workers' councils, by a general strike. It is true also that, subject to similar pressure, the principle of nationalization for coal mines was accepted, but declarations and executions are two different things. When due recognition is given to the socialist clauses and phrases in the new constitution, it remains a fact that the Social Democrats of Germany, with all their power in the state, made little or no impress upon the system of capitalist economy.

With good reason could a socialist writer lament in 1921: "The chief characteristic of our present economic condition is not only increased profits for capitalists, but the extraordinary concentration of capital in the hands of individual industrial magnates who have actually become the sovereigns of our economic life." Ebert is the president of Germany. Stinnes is the ruler of Germany.

In the other defeated countries, socialists and communists had a slight taste of power. The downfall of the old empire in Hungary was followed by the formation of a coalition government under Count Karolyi, which included three socialist ministers. This administration did not last long. Defeated in its efforts to obtain Allied aid, the Karolyi group turned the government over to the communists, headed by Bela Kun, in March, 1919. A soviet republic was then established, accompanied by great disturbances and extreme measures. It was assailed by Rumanian and Czechoslovak troops. It was attacked by a royalist faction. It was undermined by the Allied representatives in Hungary who entered into communication with the more moderate socialists and held out hopes of recognition from foreign powers in case the Kun government were ousted. On promises of immunity from prosecution, the Kun ministry retired in favor of the Social Democrats. Immediately a white terror was inaugurated which ended in the reactionary dictatorship of Admiral Horthy. The persecution and punishment of radicals was then carried to great length. Militant socialism was stamped out in blood.

In Austria, the Social Democrats played a rôle similar to that of their colleagues in Germany. Though they had opposed the declaration of war on Serbia, they came to the support of their government as soon as Russia entered the lists. If they accomplished less in the political sphere than did their brethren in Berlin, it was largely because the Austrian ministry carefully avoided calling parliament together during the early period of the war. It was only after a socialist, Adler, had shot the premier that the representatives of the people were summoned once more to take part in the government. By that time the movement in favor of peace had grown to immense proportions. In January, 1918, there was an ominous general strike. Industrial disorders, mutinies, and desertions marked the months that followed until the collapse.

In the new provisional government formed after the downfall of the monarchy, the leadership was taken by a Social Democratic premier and until the autumn of 1920 the socialists participated in the administration. During this period socialists and trade unionists were in virtual possession of the capital but the capital had been paralyzed by the disruption of the Austro-Hungarian empire. The radicals, in these circumstances, could do little more than operate the presses and print paper money. By repeated strikes they kept their wages rising with the flood of currency leaving the bourgeois to suffer as the buying power of their salaries diminished. There was, of course, a limit to this, and as time went on the socialists found out that they were helping to serve as the receivers of a bankrupt system which they could not reconstruct. Powerless even when possessing the symbols of power, they at length gave up the prerogatives of office and assumed the more congenial rôle of opposition. This may have been good party tactics, but it did not advance the socialist commonwealth of which they had so long dreamed.

III.   SOCIALISM AMONG THE VICTORS

Among the victors in the war, Italy alone witnessed an active attempt on the part of the communists to socialize industries by seizing the factories. This was not a novel thing in that kingdom. As far back as 1904, there had occurred a general strike in the north of Italy which culminated in the capture of the city of Milan by the socialists. Giolitti, who was then prime minister, refused to get excited. He would not use the troops against the strikers. In fact he employed them in preventing improvised citizen guards from attacking the radicals. His Fabian tactics proved to be successful. The strikers could cut off water, light, and power and they could seize the factories, but they found that, when they had the machinery of production without the markets, raw materials, capital, or technical leadership, they had nothing which

would produce food and clothing.   After a few days
they surrendered.

Sixteen years later, the Italian radicals made a
similar attempt with identical results.   The Socialist party of Italy adopted communist principles and
in the elections of 1919 captured 2500 communes as
against about 400 carried in the campaign of 1913.
Thus encouraged the Italian communists, in several
industrial cities, thought the time ripe to follow the
Russian example.   So they seized the factories, ex-
pelled the proprietors, and proclaimed the dictatorship of the proletariat.   Strange to say, Giolitti
was then enjoying once more a brief tenure of power
and he resorted to the tactics that had been so effective in the earlier crisis.   He shed no blood.   He let
the communists hold the undisturbed possession of
machinery and brick walls for several days until their
ardor cooled under the stress of managerial experiences.

The Italian citizens, however, were not as cool as
the government.   All over the country, self-styled
patriots, known as Fascisti, formed bands and made
war on the radicals.   There was a great deal of
street fighting and many outrages were committed
on both sides.   In this civil conflict also, the Italian
government usually assumed the rôle of a disinterested spectator.   At the close of 1921 a tentative
accord was reached between the leaders of the Fascisti and the socialists, but the rank and file have not
always observed the precise terms of the truce.

In France, the historic home of revolution, socialist enterprises since 1914 have been of a mild char-

acter. In the election of November, 1919, the socialists polled 300,000 more votes than in 1914, but owing to the operations of the new "proportional representation" law, the number of their seats in the Chamber of Deputies was cut from 101 to 65. Their strength was further dissipated by internal troubles. Long before the war there had grown up in the socialist and labor movements of France a party known as "Syndicalists" whose principles foreshadowed those of the Russian revolution of November, 1917. This group opposed parliamentary politics. It held that politicians could not transform a capitalist society into a socialist order. It declared that the revolution could only be effected by organized workingmen prepared to seize the means of production through a general strike and direct action. In practice this meant a soviet government purely economic in character. It is not surprising, therefore, that with such a movement under way, the French socialists voted in their national convention of December, 1920, to adhere to the Moscow program and the new International. The only thing approaching direct action, however, was a general railway strike which failed and called forth a decree dissolving the General Confederation of Labor. Four years of war and three years of peace left socialism and organized labor in France torn by internal dissensions and weakened in both the economic and political fields.

In contrast to the broken lines of socialism in Germany, Italy, and France, the English labor movement, once the despair of the continental social democrats, presented extraordinary unity and strength. During the war its numerical gains were large. In the election of 1911, the Labor Party candidates received 370,000 votes; in 1918 they polled 2,244,000, an immense increase even when allowance is made for woman suffrage. In addition, the Labor Party strengthened its position by adopting a carefully worked-out and moderate program which appealed to a wide constituency not identified with labor in the strict sense of the term. It announced as its aims: (1) to secure for the producers by hand and brain the full fruits of their industry and the most equitable distribution thereof that may be possible, upon the basis of common ownership of the means of production and the best obtainable system of popular administration and control of each industry or service; and (2) generally to promote the political, social, and economic emancipation of the people."

The Labor Party opposed revolution by violence and advocated the gradual application of its programme through education, political activity, co-operation, and labor organization. It announced a number of specific measures designed to guarantee a minimum of subsistence to all: democratic control of industries, a better distribution of the burdens of taxation, the prevention of vast accumulations of wealth in the hands of private parties, self-government for all peoples under British dominion, municipal and national ownership of public utilities, and peaceful relations with other nations. There was, of course, a group of Communists in England that rejected this moderate program and adopted the philosophy of Moscow, but the members of this organization were few in number and slight in influence.

The English trade unions hitherto very conservative have more than tripled their numbers since 1914 and have consolidated many of the crafts, thus taking long strides toward the realization of the "one-big-union" idea. The leaders, however, shrank from a general strike in 1921 when the miners called upon them for help in their fight against wage reductions. The paralysis of foreign trade and industry which fell upon the country in 1920 gave the labor leaders pause in their ambitious plans for united action. It may be that discretion, viewed in the large, was the better part of valor and brought strength rather than weakness to the labor movement. At all events England has witnessed no disruption and disillusionment among socialists and trade unionists comparable to the state of affairs on the continent. This may perhaps be attributed in part to the fact that the English socialists have attempted as yet no extensive application of their doctrines and in part to more astute and ambitious leadership. Still the fact stands.

IV. INTERNATIONAL SOCIALISM

The war and its aftermath had a disastrous effect upon such unity as the international socialist movement possessed before the cataclysm. The first International Working Men's Association, it is well known, had been established in 1864 with a program formulated by Karl Marx. That association lasted for twelve stormy years. It adopted a definite socialist policy in 1869, and its representatives took an active part in the Paris commune of 1871. The disaster which overwhelmed the commune, the wrath generated by the defeat, and the conflict between the socialist and the anarchist members produced a bitter internal strife in 1872 which ended in the expulsion of Bakunin, the anarchist leader, and the disruption of the Association. The socialist wing, which clung to the sinking ship, moved the headquarters to New York and after a final conference in 1876 gave up the ghost. The First International was dead and there seemed to be no possibility of resurrection.

More than ten years passed. In 1889, six years after the death of Marx, two significant international labor conferences were held in Paris and in 1891 the two bodies united. Thus the Second International came upon the scene. It admitted to membership two different groups of persons. In the first category were "all associations which adhere to the essential principles of socialism:—socialization of the means of production and exchange, international union and action of the workers, conquest of public powers by the proletariat, organized as a class party." In the second category were "all labor organizations which accept the principles of the class struggle and recognize the necessity of political action (legislative and parliamentary) but do not participate directly in the political movement." The Second International held world conferences every three or four years and maintained a permanent organization consisting of two delegates from each nation. At the general conventions socialist principles and tactics were discussed and attempts were made to draw the socialist groups of the world into ever closer unity. Many and bitter were the debates at these assemblies but by shrewd parliamentary methods and the clever use of rhetorical devices the Second International held together and seemed to grow stronger with the lapse of time.

Among the questions which agitated the Second International none was more controversial than the attitude which socialists should take toward war. The Communist Manifesto had declared: "The workers have no country. What they have not got cannot be taken from them." On this general theory, many socialists opposed all wars under all circumstances. Extremists of this type, proposed to the Second International a resolution favoring the general strike as a means of preventing war. This radical solution of the problem was hotly debated at the Stuttgart congress of 1907 and again at Copenhagen three years later. Bitter words were passed. Some German socialists, seeing the proposal supported ardently by the English socialist, Keir Hardie, even suggested that it was an English pacifist scheme to weaken the defensive power of Germany.

The outcome of the debate was a rejection of the

general strike by a vote of 131 to 51. Instead of approving this drastic anti-war weapon the convention adopted a compromise in the form of a resolution containing two parts. The first part declared that in case war threatened, the working classes and their parliamentary representatives in the countries affected, using the International Bureau as a means of coördination, should resort to "every effort to prevent war by all means which seem to them most appropriate, having regard to the sharpness of the class war and to the general political situation." The second part of the resolution declared that in case war actually broke out it would be their duty "to intervene to bring it promptly to an end, and with all their energies to use the political and economic crisis to rouse the masses of the people from their slumbers and to hasten the fall of capitalist dominion." Such was the veiled and vague language in which the socialists of the world reconciled their nationalist aspirations. Such was the official war program of the Second International in 1914.

In the last days of July, 1914, the long-dreaded black clouds were on the horizon. On July 31st, the central committee of the German Social Democrats, expecting the order for mobilization every minute, held a meeting to consider their part in the crisis. A decision was taken to send a representative to Brussels to see the secretary of the International, Huysmans, and with him to make a journey to Paris. The purpose of the expedition, according to Scheidemann, was to hold a conference with the French socialists and to reach some conclusion with reference to a common declaration in the Reichstag and the Chamber of Deputies. The conference was held during the evening of August 1st. The spokesman of the French socialists said to the German representative that the position of the two socialist groups was not the same, that the French socialists were kept fully informed as to the course of events by their government while the Germans were not, and that on the part of France it was a defensive war. The French made it clear to the German spokesman that they intended to vote for war credits and to support their government. On August 3rd, the German socialists heard the report of their representative and after a lively debate decided to sustain their own government. How much weight the report had is, of course, a matter for conjecture. There is evidence in favor of the conclusion that the decision would have been the same even though the French socialists had taken the other tack. At all events, the German socialists, like the French socialists, voted for war credits. They stuck somewhat at giving a "Hoch" for the Kaiser but were conciliated by the generous concession of the government that the "Hoch" should be for "the Kaiser, the people, and the Fatherland." The tide of war was booming in along the shore.

When the clash of resounding arms was heard in Europe, the socialist parties in several of the leading countries rallied, as did other patriot organizations to the support of their governments. This happened in England, France, Germany, Austria, and Belgium. In Russia, Serbia, Italy, Rumania,

Hungary, and the United States, however, the socialist parties officially went on record against the
war and the governments that waged it. Indeed
in all the belligerent countries there were groups
that opposed the official action of their parties,
whether for or against war. In Russia, for example, the right-wing Social Revolutionaries and Social
Democrats split off and sustained the government,
while in Germany in the course of time an intransigent group of Social Democrats broke away from
the official position of the party on the war. In
France two lines of cleavage were to be observed.
There was a very small anti-war faction. There
was a still larger group who accepted the war but
believed that socialists should not hold office in the
government during the conflict. Finally there was
the majority that favored both the war and direct
participation in the government. As the conflict
went on the opposition groups grew in size, and
during the last months of the war, a majority voted
against official coöperation within the French
ministry while still sustaining it in carrying on
hostilities.

When the war broke out, Vandervelde, the president of the International, took office in the Belgium
ministry while Huysmans, the secretary of the Bureau moved his headquarters to The Hague.
"The Second International is dead," exclaimed
Lenin, when he heard that the Social Democrats of
Germany had voted for the war credits, but Huysmans did his best to hold the retreating regiments
together. He even attempted to call a new inter-

national congress, and, defeated in that, he summoned the socialists of neutral countries to a convention held at Copenhagen in January, 1915. From this conference an appeal went forth to the socialists of the warring nations to stop the bloody conflict. The answer to this call was emphatic. The socialists of the Entente powers held a meeting in London and declared that the war must go on. The socialists of Germany, Austria, and Hungary met at Vienna, a few months later, and held an academic debate on the international relations that should prevail after the war. Against both of these patriotic conferences, the intransigent minorities opposed to war in the several countries protested in vain. If the Second International was not dead, as Lenin suggested, it was at least in mortal peril of death. At all events its temporary dissolution was patent to all mankind.

Meanwhile the minorities opposed to war were active. The Italian Socialist Party, which violently objected to Italian participation in the war and remained dead set against it to the bitter end, took the lead in welding together the opponents of the war in all countries, belligerent as well as neutral. On its initiative, a conference of the dissentients was held at Zimmerwald, in Switzerland, September, 1915. This assembly was attended by radical socialists from Russia (including Lenin and Zinoviev) Germany, France, Italy, Rumania, and some other countries. Attendance for many of them was easy for they were exiles. Representatives of the British Socialist Party and the Independent Labor party

would have gone but they were denied passports by
the English government.

The Zimmerwald conference was itself divided
into right and left wings. All were agreed in their
opposition to war and they issued an impassioned
denunciation of the belligerents. But there was a
left wing, headed by Lenin, that called for a revolution as well as an end to the war. To this the German socialist, Ledebour, replied, "It is all right for
you living here abroad to issue appeals for a civil
war. I should like to see how you would have done
it if you had lived in Russia." To this Lenin coolly
answered: "When the time arrives, we shall know
how to stand at our posts." In the spring of the
next year, another conference of the same elements
was held at Kienthal. There the extremists triumphed. A call went forth for peace and revolution. A bureau for agitation was established. The
powder train for the Russian revolution was laid.
The German Imperial Government was pleased at
the prospect of an uprising in Russia and, it seems,
aided the Russian revolutionary leaders to get back
home. At a later date the pleasure was dissolved
in tears.

Undismayed by all previous efforts and stirred
to action by the Zimmerwald-Kienthal conferences,
the officers of the Second International decided to
call a general conference at Stockholm for the summer of 1917. The March revolution in Russia
made the prospect of success more promising. The
apparent stalemate in the war made all belligerent
countries more willing to consider some way out of

the seemingly hopeless deadlock. Departing from their previous decisions, the French Socialists, the British Labor party, the German Social Democrats and the Austrian socialists voted in favor of sending delegates to Stockholm. The Petrograd Soviet, which had called for an armistice and for peace without annexations and without indemnities, greeted the occasion with congratulations. Representatives of the Zimmerwald commission migrated to Stockholm to take part in the proceedings. The stage seemed set for the extraordinary spectacle of private citizens from warring countries engaged in peace negotiations.

Naturally enough the proposal called forth violent opposition from the patriotic sections of all countries. Under the pressure of an excited public opinion, the French and British governments refused to grant passports to the delegates bound for Stockholm. As a result the convention never met. Delegates from Austria, Germany, Russia, Holland, and the Scandinavian countries appeared upon the scene, and many conferences were held among them. The German Social Democrats presented an elaborate peace program based upon the formula of no annexations and no indemnities, but after fruitless debates all the delegates gave up the enterprise as hopeless. The following year, other Inter-Allied socialists and labor conferences were called—the American Federation of Labor taking part in the last—and another statement of war aims was drafted. This however only served to emphasize the hopeless division of the Second International and to demonstrate the futility of its pacific efforts.

The failure of the Stockholm conference gave the signal to the radicals. Denouncing all "social patriots," as they called the socialists who remained loyal to their governments, the extremists decided to form a new International and to invite only revolutionary socialists to take part in it. Their plans were expedited by the triumph of the Bolsheviki in Russia. On January 24, 1919, a call for the first conference went out by wireless from Moscow to the revolutionary workers of the world. All "chauvinist socialists" were excluded from the invitation. In March, radicals from the four corners of the earth arrived in Moscow and the congress of the new association was opened. Then and there the Third International was organized and a program calling for revolution on the Russian model was adopted. At a second congress held the following year, twenty-one theses, or conditions of membership, were drafted and the revolutionary socialists of the world were called upon to adopt the orthodox creed or go into outer darkness.

These conditions were precise and admitted of little misinterpretation. "The necessity of the proletarian dictatorship" was proclaimed and adherents were required to denounce "not only the capitalists, but also their allies, the reformers of every shade and color." All the new faithful were called upon to "renounce not only social-patriotism but the false and hypocritical social-pacifism as well." All propaganda and agitation had to be of "a definite communist character and correspond to the

program and decisions of the Third International."
A relentless war on the Second International was
proclaimed and made obligatory on the new com-
munion. An iron discipline was made the rule of
life. No weaklings, no doubters, no reformers
were to be tolerated. All offices were to be filled
and all papers edited by men who deviated not a
hair's breadth from the prescribed articles of faith.
A highly centralized form of government was provided for the Third International and all members
were bound by the resolutions promulgated by the
International itself and by its executive committee.
"The Communist International has declared war
on the whole capitalist system and the old yellow
Social Democratic parties." The domestic revolution is to be wrought by a disciplined working class
not afraid of violence and dictatorship. Imperialism is to be renounced and the various countries
are to grant independence and self-government to
the dominions. Parliamentary action is to be permitted but merely as a form of propaganda. Such
was the program of the Moscow International.
Socialists of the world were called upon to accept
or reject it as a whole without quibblings or reservations. Within a few months the French Socialist party, the German Independents, a section of
the Italian Socialist party, and small socialist frag-
ments in many other countries, accepted the terms
and entered the Third International, but by that
time the power of revolutionary socialism had begun
to wane.

Meanwhile the Second International had begun

to show signs of renewed vitality. In February, 1919, a general conference was held at Berne with the representatives of nearly all the old affiliated organizations in attendance. Little was accomplished at this convention beyond a searching debate on the responsibility for the war and the merits of Bolshevik tactics. The conference went on record, however, as opposing dictatorship by a section of the working class and favoring accepted democratic methods for establishing the socialist order. A second convention, held at Geneva during the next year, worked out a new and elaborate statement of socialist aims and tactics, following the program of the British Labor Party rather than that of Moscow. The dictatorship of the proletariat was utterly rejected and the methods and processes of modern democracy were declared appropriate and essential to the realization of a socialist commonwealth. At the same time, the idea of a vocational parliament, representing trades and professions, was endorsed on the understanding that ultimate sovereignty must rest in the political assembly elected by universal suffrage.

After the Geneva conference of 1920, negotiations were started for a union of the two internationals. Moscow became less pontifical. The right wing moderated its criticism. On April 2, 1922, representatives of the Second and the Third Internationals, with spokesmen for the middle group, known as the Two-and-one-half International, met in the Reichstag Building in Berlin and adopted provisional measures looking toward a reunion.

V. INTERNATIONAL TRADE
UNIONISM

In making a survey of the labor movement as a whole it is necessary to distinguish sharply between the socialist or political phase and straight trade unionism. By no means all the trade unionists of the world were socialists in 1914. In America and in England relatively few of them were. In Germany the unions were divided into groups according to their political affiliations. There were, for example, Social Democratic unions and Catholic unions. In spite of their great divergences in politics, however, the trade unions of the various countries often coöperated closely in economic and political battles and they were united in a grand International Federation of Trade Unions, formed at Copenhagen in 1901. This world organization was able to hold together and function only by abstaining from debates about controversial political and social questions. It declared that the object of its conferences was "to consider the closer union of the trade unions of all countries, uniform trade union statistics, mutual help in economic struggles, and all questions in direct connection with trade union organization of the workers." It was expressly agreed that "all theoretical questions and those which affect the tendency or tactics of the trade union movement in the separate nations will not be discussed." Under this program 7,394,-000 trade unionists were federated in 1912, those of the United States being included.

During the Great War, this International Federation of Trade Unions was practically dormant, although a few conferences of neutrals were held. In fact it was split along definite lines. There was a Central Powers section, an Allied section, and a neutral section. In these circumstances nothing could be accomplished. Within the several nations, however, the trade unions made strides in seven league boots. Their numbers were immensely increased. In Germany the membership affiliated with the International rose from 2,553,000 in 1912 to 8,500,000 in 1920. In Great Britain the affiliated membership grew from 874,000 to 6,500,000 during the same period. In the meantime the trade unionists had augmented their powers through the terms and conditions which they had been able to wring from the belligerent governments. In a war of steel and chemicals, the producers and carriers of goods are as essential as the soldiers at the front—and not subjected to the same iron discipline. So the trade unions of Europe emerged from the war more numerous and more influential than ever.

Shortly after the signature of the Treaty at Versailles in 1919, the dismantled International Trade Union Federation was restored to working order. The new organization, contrary to tradition, did not restrict itself to unionism pure and simple. It called for a complete program of labor legislation, for the socialization and international control of raw materials, and for radical measures against war in the future. It favored "international mass action in the assault on reaction, in declaring war against war, and for the realization of a new social system." This was too extreme for Mr. Samuel Gompers, head of the American Federation of Labor, and he carried his organization out of the world Federation, denouncing it in round terms. On the other hand, it was too conservative for Moscow; so the Russian unions proceeded to form a "revolutionary international trade union organization." This effort bore little fruit. The regular International announced that its membership in 1920 without the United States was 23,662,000 against a membership of 7,394,000 in 1912 when it included the 2,000,000 American unionists. The "Red" trade union international seems to have made no gains worthy of record.

VI.   SOME GENERAL REFLECTIONS

After this general survey, it must be conceded that it is perilous to draw any very large conclusions as to the present status of the socialist and labor movements throughout the world. Over against slight retrocessions in political strength in some countries must be set immense gains in others. Organized labor has multiplied its membership more than four fold bringing up the world total to nearly thirty millions. Notwithstanding the so-called "liquidation of labor" during the business crisis, there has been no such reduction in membership as has occurred in previous panics. The international organization of trade unionists is far more radical in its economic views than before the Great War and labor from only one country, the

United States, rejects its program. If the failures of communism in Russia, Italy, and Hungary and the shortcomings of the Social Democrats in Germany and Austria seem to warrant the rejection of socialism as an impossible dream, the voters in the working class quarters of Europe do not seem to have discovered it. It may be, as many writers contend, that Karl Marx is dead; but the rejoinder may also be made with equal force that Cobden and Bright are dead also.

It is doubtless true that a large number of socialists who hoped to spring into the millenium by means of a sudden revolution have been disillusioned. It is equally true that there has come about as a result of the past seven years' experience a thoroughgoing reorganization of socialist thought. When socialists were mere obstructionists and opponents, they could talk grandly about the great day in the distant future when the coöperative commonwealth was to be established. Their programs had little relation to reality. Their platforms had never been shaped with reference to the contingency of an actual revolution that would sweep socialists into power. Their manifestos usually consisted of two parts. In one part were included their immediate demands, such as the eight hour day, universal suffrage, and other "bourgeois reforms." In the other part, in somewhat pontifical style, appeared the philosophy of inevitability—the revelation of the joyful day when the death knell of capitalism would be rung out and the new world would be born in the shell of the old. If anyone, of a practical turn of mind, asked what actually would be done on that great day, he was set down as a doubter in the house of the faithful. He was answered by references to "natural processes," "the disappearance of the state," and "the end of class distinctions." "In the place of the old bourgeois society," ran the prophecy of the Communist Manifesto, "with its classes and class antagonisms, an association appears in which the free development of each is the condition for the free development of all."

When, however, Ebert, Scheidemann, Lenin, Trotzky, and their comrades were swept into power by forces not conjured up by their oratory, they found the great day at hand and with it taxes to collect, pay rolls to meet, railways to manage, factories to operate, and few hundred thousand other things to do. In all the vast range of socialist literature there was scarcely a hint as to the line of actual conduct to pursue. Such was the irony of fate that they had to turn to capitalist rather than to socialist literature for guidance. They laid Marx on the shelf and took a course in the Taylor system of efficiency management. They found that the wrath of man might praise the Creator but could not produce a potato or move a freight engine. Rhetoric does not build houses. Party programs do not make plows. Logic, philosophy, and Hegelianism do not install power plants. The socialists learned that they had been thinking in terms of the old politics and the old statescraft and that the possession of the pomp and circumstances of power did not automatically set in motion the complex productive processes of national life. The effect of this experience, bitter and disillusioning as it was, had a deep influence upon socialist thought.

This influence can be traced fully in the economic literature of Germany since 1918. Before the revolution, the German socialists seldom used the word "socialization," and perhaps never the verb "socialize." Now *Socialisierung* is the order of the day. The failures in Russia and Germany forced the Socialists to accept the bourgeois challenge to produce evidences of practical power and practical understanding, and they have been busy recasting their literature. They are writing on exactly how industries may be taken over by society, organized, managed, and made more productive. They are discussing the rôle of workers councils, technicians, entrepreneurs, and capitalists. They are writing on foreign trade, productivity, wages under socialism, the distribution of output, autonomous industrial corporations, the dangers of bureaucracy, vertical and horizontal trusts, finance, transportation, and agriculture. There is now a new note of reality in their speculations. They know by experience that the red flag may proudly wave over a starving population and all power does not proceed from occupants of swivel chairs in government buildings.

What will be the effect of this? Who can answer? One or two suggestions may be ventured. As the socialists lay aside the rhetoric of academic philosophy and politics and adopt the language of production and management, they will be writing and talking about things which capitalists and businessmen can understand.   Their ideas will begin to circulate in spheres hitherto closed to them.   If there is reality in what they have to say, if there is force of fact behind their argument, they cannot fail to produce a profound impression on the economic thought of all classes.   On the other hand, this very process of hard thinking about reality, will itself have a disintegrating influence upon the pontifical assurance of socialist dogma.   Thus the philosophy of capitalism and socialism will have new points of contact and a larger spirit of compromise may enter into the contests of the future.

Whatever may be the influence of social philosophy upon the conduct of human affairs, two facts appear indelibly upon the record of the recent past. When the ruling classes of two great empires— Russia and Germany—went into bankruptcy as the outcome of the First World War, it was only socialist parties that had the power and will and organization necessary to seize and hold the government.   Those who are given, with Volney, to meditations upon the ruins of states will be moved to speculate upon the possible rôle of socialism and organized labor at the end of the Tenth World War.

IX

AMERICA AND THE BALANCE OF POWER

"IN the beginning was the deed," wrote the wise poet. Activity yet remains the essential thing in the life of mankind. Political speeches, addresses on foreign policies, and Fourth of July orations exert little influence on the course of human affairs, save occasionally in time of a crisis when the spoken word indicates a line of action to be followed. The fate of a nation—its destiny—lies not in words but in deeds. The nation lives by work not by rhetoric. It is no detraction from the high honor rightly ascribed to the Fathers of this republic to say that, well as they built, they alone did not make America. Our America was made by the pioneers, men and women, who levelled the forests, laid out the roads, tilled the fields, and carried American life to the Pacific, and by the capitalists and laborers who constructed and operated the steel mills with their roaring furnaces and the spinning mills with their flying spindles. I do not mean to say that concepts of life and duty do not underlie this fabric of human endeavour, but merely that the majestic signs of power are the outcome of activity.

So, whoever fain would divine the fate of a nation must ponder deeply its activity. It is not what we say about the sea that counts; it is what our sailors do upon the seas. It is not our academic theories about finance that carry weight in the councils of nations; it is our dollars and our cents that imperatively command the attention and wholesome respect of those engaged in the counting houses of the earth's great cities. It is not what President Harding thinks about China or what John Hay has written about China that will shape the coming fateful years in the Pacific; it is what our merchants, our capitalists, our railway builders, and our money lenders do in China that will set the problem for the rising generation.

Now America is primarily an industrial and a trading nation. Its prime activities are connected with the production and sale of goods. It has no landed nobility to cultivate the graces of leisure. It has no military aristocracy devoted to the exercise of arms. Napoleon once sneered at the nation of shopkeepers, but it was the sneer of jealousy, and the Anglo-Saxon is proud of the term of contempt thus flung at him. Whether this pride is warranted or not, whether the virtues of trade—those bourgeois virtues so scorned of the emancipated—are really virtues, is a matter for the theologian and the ethical teacher. The fact remains. America is an industrial and trading nation. Our activities at home and abroad are mainly related to these essential elements in our national life. Here then is the key to our domestic history and to our future foreign policies. Our empire of trade extends to the four corners of the world. It stretches out under many flags and many governments. Those working at its periphery, under the pressure of economic laws, make the conditions with which American foreign policy must deal. They create the stern and solemn facts with which statesmen and politicians must reckon.

Moreover, recent circumstances have given a new turn to the significance of business. Many nations of antiquity in the course of their history came to rely upon the food supplies brought from distant lands. Rome in her imperial days was fed by wheat carried from her uttermost provinces; when this supply was cut off and the fields of Italy failed to make good the shortage, the staff of life failed. The new nations and new states that rose upon the foundations of Rome were almost self-sufficing. At all events they could feed their population by food grown within their own borders. With the advent of the machine age, this fortunate condition was lost by the leaders in invention and manufacture. In 1914 neither England nor Germany could maintain a standard of living for the laboring population without drawing heavily upon the granaries of America and Russia. The huge populations, called into being by the opportunities of industry, constituted a growing pressure upon the agencies of business and of government compelling them to extend and maintain foreign markets. This naturally drove the seekers for markets into the backward places of the earth where industry had not penetrated or had made little advance. For nearly a century England had no formidable rival in this imperial enterprise, then one after another competitors appeared upon the world stage—Germany, Japan, Italy, France, and the United States. Even in China and India the whirr of the spindle and the clank of the loom were heard ringing out the fate of Lancashire cotton mills. Here were the roots of imperialism, armaments, and warfare. Those who asked where this all would finally lead and what would be the outcome when every nation became industrial were silenced by the inexorable demands of current business. After us the deluge!

In this swiftly drifting world economy, the United States occupies a peculiar position. From one point of view it is very fortunate. It can feed its immense population with almost every kind of product from oranges and sugar to wheat and bacon. It can clothe its people with the cotton of the South and, did exigencies again demand, with wool from the sheep ranges. Considered abstractly it could be a self-sufficing nation. But considered practically, it is, as things now stand, dependent upon foreign trade, if not for a livelihood, at least for what is called "prosperity." It is the city populations of England and Germany that must have markets abroad and import food supplies. In the United States, the wheat and corn grower of the West, the cotton grower of the South, as well as the maker of silks in Patterson or the manufacturer of steel in Pittsburg, all depend upon foreign business for that margin of trade which spells prosperity. In short having an endowment of agricultural resources beyond the strength of our domestic markets for the produce we must perforce sell the foreigner foodstuffs as well as boots and clothes. Here is a paradox which seems to have received small attention from professional economists.

In every respect, the World War has increased the dependence of the United States upon world markets even for the profitable disposal of its surplus capital. It has discharged a very large portion of its indebtedness abroad and has become an insistent money lender itself. In 1915, European capitalists held $2,704,000,000 worth of American railway stocks and securities; two years later more than half of these holdings had been transferred to America; and the stream still continues to flow westward. In 1914 more than one-fourth of the stocks of the United States Steel Corporation were held in Europe; today less than one tenth are in foreign hands. The crisis induced in London, long the money center of the world, by the exigencies of the war, led to the phenomenal rise of New York. To sustain their credit here for huge borrowings, England and France opened their strong boxes and sent across the sea the very finest of their gilt edge securities. As a keen French economist puts it: "One fact dominates all others: the rise of the United States to world hegemony. Lord Robert Cecil has compared the position of the United States after the Great War with that of Great Britain after the Napoleonic wars. That comparison is not quite exact; because the British hegemony was then essentially European while that of the United States today is universal. An immense reservoir of raw materials, of manufactured products, and of capital, the United States has become an economic centre and financial centre in connection with which all the world must work and trade." Fact, stern, and tremendous as Carlyle might say, indubitable and fateful. Beside it all rhetoric fails. The loom on which is woven the texture of world politics has been brought across the sea and the picks of its flashing shuttle can be counted in the financial columns of any great New York daily.

The United States has, therefore, entered upon the rôle long played by England and France as an international banker and money lender. The visible signs of these new activities are the numerous American banking houses which are to be found in the principal streets and squares of European cities. The Morgan House and the Bankers Trust Company look upon the monument erected to Napoleon's glories in Place Vendome. If you will turn to the financial section of such a metropolitan paper as the New York *Times,* you will see the statistical record of American operations in foreign finance. Only recently the transactions in foreign government bonds upon the Stock Exchange have become so great as to require a separate section of the daily statement. Often such transactions occupy one-fourth of the space given to the day's record. The list of bonds bought and sold on a single day is both interesting and full of meaning. The list includes Argentine, Chinese Railway, City of Berne, Bordeaux, Christiania, Copenhagen, Lyons, Marseilles, Rio de Janeiro, Tokio, Zürich, Danish Municipalities, Department of the Seine, Dominican Republic, Dominion of Canada, Dutch East Indies, French Government, Japanese Government, Belgium, Denmark, Italy, Sweden, Chile, Cuba, Uruguay, San Paulo, Queensland, Rio Grande do Sul, Swiss Confederation, United Kingdom of Great Britain and Ireland, Brazil, and Haiti, not to mention the defaulted securities of Russia and Mexico. When to the sales of these government bonds are added the transactions in the currency and bonds of Central and Eastern European powers and the transactions in the stocks and obligations of foreign industrial corporations, it becomes apparent that American investors are deeply involved in the fate of governments and enterprises in all parts of the world. Almost every week records the floating of a new loan to some foreign city or country or railway already staggering under a burden of debt. The rates are high, the commissions enormous, and the risks correspondingly great.

In accordance with a custom, consecrated by time, the bondholders, whenever a disturbance is threatened or a default is at hand, look eagerly to the government at Washington to support their interests diplomatically if not more vigorously. The genial American public, that takes up millions of oil stocks every year, seizes eagerly at the opportunity to get seven and eight per cent on the bonds of foreign countries and so every new loan is received with enthusiasm. Let this process go on for fifty years, and the people of the United States will have reconditioned Europe and Asia, and at the same time created an interest obligation that will either flood our markets with European goods by way of repayment, or raise the dollar to a ruinous height in the exchanges of the world. They will also have incurred a gigantic financial risk which a new war or a social revolution in Europe would transform into widespread ruin with its corresponding effects on our political issues. In short, the United States, through the investment of capital, has become a silent partner in the fate of every established order in the world. Unless we are to assume on the basis of the experience of the past three hundred years that there will be no more World Wars or social cataclysms, it is safe to conjecture that days of greater trouble are ahead, whether we enter the League of Nations or stay out of it. Once a great European war merely deranged our foreign trade; in the future it will disturb every investor in every village Main Street. Entangling political alliances may be pieces of paper, as the past has shown, but the texture of the economic alliance is woven of tougher materials. Politics comes after the fact. The gilt-edged pieces of parchment handed out to American investors will speak louder than the silver tongues of professional orators.

In industry, as in finance, the upward swing of the United States after 1914 was incredible in its swiftness and majestic in its range. Our old competitors in Europe were not only paralysed by war activities; they clamored louder and louder for the products of American mills, mines, and factories. Measured in tons of steel, pounds of copper, and bolts of cloth, the sales of the United States abroad between 1914 and 1918 were nothing short of staggering. We supplied not only belligerents in Europe, but their former customers in South America, Asia, and the islands of the seas. Colossal factories sprang up on our soil. Old plants were enlarged and extended. Thousands of new workers were drawn into the cities from the countryside, especially as immigration fell off. American capital was amassed in stupendous quantities and preparations were made to seize the empire of world trade. Having an immense home market with the corresponding advantages of large-scale production, American business men prepared to lead the world in industry and finance. They were even able to induce a Democratic Congress, in spite of its inveterate suspicion, to enact the Webb law authorizing the formation of gigantic combinations to develop and exploit foreign markets.

In the normal course of things, if the history of England and Germany is our guide, a merchant marine and sea power follow the growth of foreign business. In this sphere also the trend of American economic development is true to form. On the eve of the World War, the American merchant marine was an almost negligible factor upon the high seas. It is true that long ago our wooden ships were upon every ocean and our sailors rivalled in skill and daring the best upon the wave; but the glory of our enterprise upon the waters vanished during the Civil War. After 1865 the record of nearly every year showed a decline. In 1861

American ships brought to our shores more than one-half, in values, of all the goods imported; in 1913 they carried only about eleven per cent of the values. Meanwhile the tonnage of ships for oceanic trade fell from 2,547,000 to 1,928,999 reducing the United States to a position below that of England, Germany, and Norway. During the same period the proportion of exports carried from our shores in American ships dropped from seventy-two per cent in values to nine per cent. Americans, busy with the development of their continent, and content with their lake and coastwise trade, let foreign ships carry their exports and imports. The planters and farmers of the country rejected every proposal to build a merchant marine by national subsidies—the only device which American capitalists could offer as a means of bringing the ocean carrying trade into American hands.

So things stood in 1914 when the war drove the German merchant marine from the seas and compelled the other belligerents to commandeer ships for military purposes. Then the United States found itself in the presence of a crisis similar to that induced by the Napoleonic wars. One hundred years before, cotton, tobacco, corn, and bacon from American plantations and farms lay wasting at the docks for want of ships to carry them abroad. In 1914, the owners of vast masses of manufactured goods as well as the owners of farm produce clamored for ships. Thus it happened that the Democratic party, which many years before had withdrawn subsidies from the American marine, found itself confronted by a trying situation. The cry for ships went up on every hand. It was no longer the steel makers and the owners of ship yards alone that were heard in the lobbies of Congress. The munition makers needed ships. The farmers and planters needed them. So the Democratic party, the party of the less government the better, like all parties, laid aside theories in the presence of compelling facts and set about creating an American marine. Without utterly repudiating the teachings of half a century, it could not openly resort to the subsidies and bounties it had so long and so passionately denounced. But the ships had to be built. There was another alternative. The government itself could go into ship building. In 1916, the Shipping Board was created for that purpose. Soon the war came to America. Then with lavish grants from the public treasury ships were built with a speed that astonished the world.

Thanks to what appears to be a historical accident, the United States has now become one of the great oceanic carrying powers. In 1914 our ship yards turned out 200,000 tons of shipping while those of Great Britain turned out 1,683,000 tons. In 1918, our yards launched 3,000,000 tons while the English yards set afloat 1,348,000 tons. All around our long coast lines American ingenuity was applied with astounding zeal and marvellous results. The experiment was costly, for money was spent like water, but "the goods were delivered." Within the course of five years the American flag was restored to its old preëminence on the high seas.

In the Atlantic and the Pacific new steamship lines made their appearance bidding for freight and passenger business. New shipping offices were opened in all the chief ports of the world. An ever increasing proportion of our exports and imports was carried in American bottoms. The steamship companies of Europe found themselves face to face with a new and formidable competitor. In 1920 the total number of American vessels, registered as engaged in foreign trade and whale fishing, showed a tonnage of 9,928,595, to say nothing of the 6,395,-429 tons engaged in coastwise and internal trade. In 1918 the entire merchant marine of the United Kingdom amounted to 10,000,000 tons in round numbers. Thus it happened when the war stopped that the world was overstocked with merchant vessels and in every harbor steamers and sailing ships lay rusting and rotting. Then the great cry went up that the government which by lavish expenditures had built the ships should subsidize those into whose hands they passed at a nominal cost. With the economics of this great transaction, we are not concerned. The striking fact is established that the United States has become within six years one of the first oceanic carriers of the world, a formidable competitor of all the maritime nations.

Coincident with this growth in the merchant marine was a tremendous stride forward in battleship construction. Until the Spanish war, America was not reckoned among the great sea powers, although her sailors had given a good account of themselves in many contests upon the ocean. After Manila Bay and Santiago, however, increasing attention was given to the navy and in 1914 the United States ranked third in naval strength. Then began a period of feverish activity marked by constantly increasing acceleration. In 1920, the Navy General Board reported its grand designs: "A navy second to none recommended by the General Board in 1915 is still required today. But in addition the great war has shown the importance of unimpeded ocean transportation for commerce. If either belligerent loses the control of the sea, the national fighting power and endurance are greatly affected. In time of peace a great and developing country needs a proportionately great merchant fleet of its own to insure its markets and preserve its commerce from subservience to rival nations and their business." That report struck home and its spirit was reflected in the new building program. So rapid was American progress that experts were able to calculate that by 1926 the fighting power of the United States on the sea would surpass that of Great Britain. The long supremacy inaugurated in the defeat of the *Armada* was on the verge of passing to America when the Washington conference called a halt in competitive armaments.

So out of the World War emerged a new America, first among the investing, industrial, commercial, maritime, and naval powers of the earth—a country endowed with an immense productive equipment and ready to penetrate the most inaccessible markets of the most distant lands. At the same time, a paralysis of Europe cut down the demand for American agricultural produce and manufactured goods, and the destruction of the Russian and German empires gave a new and startling turn to events in the Orient, leaving Japan without the support of any great power save England. It was inevitable, amid these circumstances, that we should witness a burst of American activity in the Far East.

This is of course a new emphasis rather than a new factor for Oriental trade had been an important element in American economy and politics since the maturity of the Pacific seaboard states, especially since the acquisition of the Philippines and the opening of the Panama canal. The Pacific has become the new theatre. It has been said that the drama of antiquity was played on the shores of the Mediterranean and that the drama of the modern world has been enacted on the shores of the Atlantic. The drama of the future is preparing on a more majestic stage where teeming millions stand ready to take part in it. The curtain has risen upon this new drama. The actors are in their places, but no living mind can divine even the first act to say nothing of the dénouement. Asia is old, wise, fertile in ideas and rich in potential resources. It had its empires, its religions and philosophies long before the geese cackled on the banks of the Tiber. Many conquerors have tried their fortunes there. England has brought the vast southern peninsula under her imperial dominion, but her subjects stir ominously and the solid structure may in time dissolve. Japan, aroused from her lethargy by Yankee enterprise, is equipped in wealth, industrial power, and military strength to extend and defend her mighty hegemony. China, huge, amorphous, beset by a thousand ills, threatened with dissolution, and restless under the influence of western ideas lies prostrate but, having survived a hundred conquests and conquerors, may yet smile in her enigmatic way upon the Lilliputians who assail her. Russia, at present broken and powerless, seems out of the play, but that is an illusion except to those who reckon human affairs in terms of flags and states. The Russian people multiply with the passing years and they push out upon the Asiatic plains with the relentless force of an Alpine glacier. Those who occupy the earth and till the soil at their feet will in the long run possess it. Russia, the land of Tolstoi and Lenin and Sazonov and Nicholas Romanov, still lives and will again play a leading part in the drama that unrolls in the Pacific basin.

The first speeches of the American actors have already been delivered. The policy of "the Open Door" has been announced. It has an immense advantage. It has an ethical ring. It respects the integrity, sovereignty, and territory of the Chinese nation. It contemplates no military aggression, no forcible annexations, no political power. It merely asks that all nations have equal rights to go and come, buy and sell, invest and collect in China. In theory it corresponds to the modern ideal of free commerce, though it may mean that in practice immense monopolies may be built up, monopolies such as have arisen in Europe and the United States out of the same freedom of commerce. In theory it meets the approval of China, for China, naturally anxious to preserve her territorial unity against foreign domination, welcomes assistance. While thus corresponding to China's immediate desires and expressing an ethical doctrine, the open door policy also satisfies the practical interests of the United States, at present. The seizure and government of Chinese territory would involve difficulties, financial and administrative; if opportunities of trade may be secured without this hazard, territorial annexations would be exercises in foolhardiness.

The belief in our own disinterestedness in the pursuit of the open-door policy is so wide-spread that any opposition to it on the part of other countries concerned in the Orient is viewed as a manifestation of unwarranted ill-will. Undoubtedly American policy offers a striking contrast to the policy of penetration and aggression followed by many other powers. Nevertheless, it does not appear to be entirely benevolent to the seasoned diplomats of the Old World, as the papers recently published from the Russian archives show. In these papers, the American State Department is represented as aiding vigorously in the economic penetration of China and as supporting American banks with interests hostile to those of the other powers. It is not necessary to accept these criticisms at face value or on the basis of them to entertain doubts as to the correctness of American diplomacy. That is not the point. The heart of the matter is that neither Europeans nor the Japanese look upon American imperial methods in the Orient as different in any essential respect from those of other powers. The American goal, they say, is the same, namely, opportunities for profitable trade and investment, and as the Philippines bear witness, territorial expansion is not avoided when it becomes necessary. The spirit of cynicism and doubt as to the ultimate intentions of America in the East, though we may vigorously condemn it, must nevertheless be understood if we are to gauge correctly forces of the future. Nowhere is this spirit more accurately reflected than in an article by an eminent French publicist, in the *Mercure de France,* for January, 1922. This single passage gives the heart of the matter:

"The realist, the positive, and especially the financial, mentality which is the true characteristic of the Yankee and his raison d'être, has been profoundly stirred by the situation created in the United States during and after the war—a situation which he had not foreseen and which is presented under the form of a genuine paradox. Enriched in that conflict to the point of securing almost all the gold of the world, North America nevertheless is passing through a crisis of appalling proportions; unemployment, a paralysis of the export trade, and all the economic calamities, now oppressing American citizens, fell upon them at the same time as an exceptionally favorable state of exchange and an unexpected abundance of treasure. It occurred at once to the minds of these practical men that it was necessary henceforward to secure a market other than that afforded by Europe, a field of action in which their preponderant or semi-sovereign influence will permit them to sell their products and their primary materials under conditions of exchange which they will regulate themselves. Thus they will avoid as far as possible the economic laws which, in their operation, have become so dangerous for them in Europe. Since they were powerless in Europe to regulate the value of money which depends upon a number of circumstances—upon a state of affairs peculiar to the Old World and beyond their control, —it was urgent that they should have at their disposal an Asiatic country where they could act, direct, and organize at their pleasure and where their commerce would not encounter the same perils as among their old customers. China is there, immense and ready, they think, to receive all authorities, and so disorganized that she is ready to accept anything they wish to impose upon her. Hence there were, even during the war, missions of all sorts, economic, financial, religious, educational, and recreational sailing from Frisco to the Middle Kingdom.

"At that moment, Japan began to be disturbed. For other reasons than the United States, even for opposite reasons, Japan felt the need of extending her influence over the great Yellow Republic; above all for reasons connected with natural resources. Wanting in coal and iron, Japan must of necessity possess these things without depending upon any powerful nation. Moreover her seventy-seven million people are crowded into a country about as large as France and at any price it was necessary to search for an outlet for emigrants. In short, with the United States established in

China, there was at her gate an enemy which had shown a tenacious hatred for her and an unchanging contempt for the yellow race, since, according to the Yankee conception of things, the yellow man, who is only a charming being when one visits him to get his money, becomes intolerable when he asks for simple reciprocity. . . . Mr. Hughes has proposed that the American republic should dominate the Pacific—twenty-eight million more inhabitants than Japan to undertake the economic conquest of China, eight super-battleships more than the Mikado possesses to curb his desires—there are the powerful trump cards, and if America succeeds in making them serve her purpose, she will have a beautiful party. Although officially disinterested for the moment in the affairs of Europe, she sees that they are being reintegrated secretly in general policy through financiers who meet in their private chambers and associate with themselves at the council table some Anglo-Saxon business men and some Germans who more than ever divide the world." Such is a view of American policy now, by an eminent French publicist. How much untruth there is in it each may decide for himself according to his knowledge. Now that we have set out upon the way it is wise to see ourselves as our critics see us, for it is our critics, not our friends, who will make trouble for us.

Whether we accept or reject the criticisms of the French observer, we cannot overlook the fact that the widely-heralded Washington conference was related mainly, even almost exclusively, to Pacific, not European, problems. Though associated in the minds of some with various world enterprises such as the League of Nations, it was in fact confined in its chief activities to the practical adjustment of Pacific matters in such a way as to facilitate the prosperity of American trade. When the conference was first called, many enthusiasts began to see visions of general disarmament and universal peace, but President Harding sharply reminded them that nothing of the sort was contemplated. He had in view reducing the cost of warlike preparations in time of peace, to the great relief of the burdened taxpayers, and settling certain specific matters likely to cause friction among the powers concerned. The two projects were closely knit in the realm of fact. As President Harding said in his address to the Senate on February 9, 1922, in submitting the results of the conference to that body: "Much as it was desirable to lift the burdens of naval armament and strike at the menace of competitive construction and consequent expenditures, the Executive branch of the Government, which must be watchful for the Nation's safety, was unwilling to covenant a reduction of armament until there could be plighted new guarantees of peace, until there could be removed probable menaces of conflict." After this plain declaration of prosaic fact, President Harding went to the heart of the matter. "We have seen the eyes of the world," he said, "turned to the Pacific. With Europe prostrate and penitent, none feared the likelihood of early conflict there. But the Pacific had its menaces and they deeply concerned us. Our territorial interests are larger there. Its waters are not strange seas to us, its farther shores not unknown to our citizens. . . . We covet the possessions of no other power in the Far East and we know for ourselves that we crave no further or greater governmental or territorial responsibilities there. Contemplating what is admittedly ours, and mindful of a long-time and reciprocal friendship with China, we do wish the opportunity to continue the development of our trade peacefully and on equality with other nations." When all the rhetoric, ceremonials, and formalities are laid aside, there is the sum and substance of the whole business. "The Pacific had its menaces and they deeply concerned us."

What were those menaces in fact and deed? Who made those menaces? No informed person is under any delusions on this matter. Russia, long the aggressor and high chief engineer of intrigues against Chinese territory, is paralyzed and powerless for the present and the indefinite future. France, though possessed of a huge Indo-Chinese empire, offers no serious challenge. Germany is bankrupt in military power and can do no more than make commercial gestures. There remain England and Japan. They are the only powers in a position to encroach upon Chinese territorial integrity, and in 1921 these two powers were bound by an alliance. "The Pacific had its menaces." They were real; they were two-fold; they were united, and the United States at the same time had no intention of surrendering any of the opportunities of American merchants, manufacturers, and financiers in China.

Thus it happened that the desires of the tax-payers for relief and the pacific aspirations of the American people, coincided with a genuine crisis in the far eastern relations of the American Government. For eight years conditions had been abnormal. President Wilson, as the spokesman of planters, farmers, and trade unions, did not continue the aggressive policy pursued by the Secretary of State, Philander Knox, in the advancement of American trading and investing interests in the East. Moreover the war had dislocated forces, engaged the energies of England, paralyzed Russia, eliminated Germany, and given Japan a free hand. In fact between the retirement of President Taft and the inauguration of President Harding, Japan had made immense strides in the extension of her hegemony over China. At first she operated in conjunction with Russia, with the consent of England. Then in the midst of the war, Japan made her famous Twenty-one Demands which in effect promised to destroy the remnants of Chinese sovereignty. Mr. Wilson, so zealous in the interest of universal peace and the League of Nations, approved the Lansing-Ishü doctrine, let Shantung go to Japan, and neglected Yap.

It is in the light of these things that the results of the Washington conference must be examined. First, there is the naval holiday and the Four Power treaty. As all conversant with naval affairs know, by 1924 or 1926 at the latest, according to the prevalent rate of construction the United States

would have been supreme at sea over Great Britain
in fighting units and weight of metal. But Great
Britain was united to Japan by a treaty of alliance
and the two constituted a formidable power. By
offering debt-burdened Britain a relief in naval construction the United States induced her to cut loose
from a separate alliance with Japan. Hence the
naval holiday. It is an immense gain to the tax
payers. It gives experts time to study the whole
question of sea fighting in view of the great prob-
ability that Dreadnoughts and Super-Dreadnoughts
are as obsolete as wooden walls.

The accompanying Four Power treaty is likewise
susceptible of many interpretations as to origin, purpose, and implications. The terms of the instrument are very general. The high contracting
parties agree to respect one another's insular possessions in the Pacific and to enter into communication in case any disturbance arises in that connection. On its face that declaration appears to be a
truism. President Harding informed the Senate
and the country that "nothing in any of these
treaties commits the United States or any other
power to any kind of alliance, entanglement or en-
volvement." But as if baffled by his own statement, he added: "It has been said, if this be true,
these are meaningless treaties and therefore value-
less. Let us accept no such doctrine of despair as
that." It has been stated, but not officially, that the
purpose of the Four Power treaty was to destroy
the Anglo-Japanese alliance and if this is true the
somewhat uncertain terms become full of meaning.

At all events the way is made clear for the pursuit of the open-door trading policy in China.

More precise is the treaty laying down the principles to be pursued with regard to China. The high contracting parties once more proclaim the sovereignty, the independence, the territorial and administrative integrity of China, and free and equal opportunity for commerce and industry. They agree that they will not seek or support their nationals in seeking: (a) any arrangement which might purport to establish in favor of their interests any general superiority of right with respect to commercial or economic development in any designated regions of China; (b) any such monopoly or preference as would deprive the nationals of any other power of the right of undertaking any legitimate trade or industry in China or of participating with the Chinese government or with any local authority in any category of public enterprise, or which by reason of its scope, duration, or geographical extent is calculated to frustrate the practical application of the principle of equal opportunity.

Two things are to be noted about this treaty. The language, though perhaps as specific as circumstances admitted, is nevertheless general in character. It is open to a variety of interpretations in the application. It is less specific and pointed than the language of the famous Algeciras compact which was supposed to put an end to friction among the powers in Morocco. It does not contain the detailed provisions, limitations, prohibitions, and specifications laid down in 1906 for the conduct of the Sultan's estate. That is the first point to be noted. The second is that it is, like the Algeciras compact, applicable to a country in disorder and revolution, to a rapidly changing situation, not to a settled society like the United States or England where commerce can be carried on without recourse to armed force. When France was reproached with having torn up the compact of Algeciras, she could with justice reply that local conditions were such that its application, according to the ordinary norms of legal procedure, was impossible. So it was.

CONCLUSIONS

Any one who has given two or three years to the study of the course of affairs in Europe since 1918 will hesitate to advance with firm assurance very many "conclusions." The pages which follow should really be entitled "A Few General and Tentative Reflections." Europe is in an unstable equilibrium and serious changes may take place any moment. Generalizations are dangerous. Prophecy is more dangerous. But the human mind longs for something more positive than a glimpse at a swirling tide. Hence these last words.

The first reflection is perhaps the easiest to formulate. There are many signs of European recovery in the realm of fact. The reconstruction work in France has been truly marvellous. The basic industry, agriculture, though disturbed by agrarian changes in Eastern Europe, is being restored and a decided turn upward may be expected shortly. The quarrels among the new nationalities are being allayed by negotiations and treaties and new bonds of trade and intercourse are taking the place of those snapped by the war. In this sphere time will bring healing.

Secondly, finance and industry in Europe are in a state of chaos and conditions are growing worse rather than better. If the analysis given in Chapter IV is sound, it is difficult to see how business can be brought to its old course without reducing reparations and inter-allied debts, scaling down domestic debts, and restoring the currency to a gold basis. Europe must soon choose between some kind of a general economic constitution and a re-alignment of powers for more costly and deadly conflicts.

Thirdly, the principle of conscious and systematic support for commercial enterprise has been adopted by England, France, Germany, and Italy, and the capitalists of these countries are driving forward to the conquest of new markets with a greater zeal than in the days before the war. There is this difference: they are more effectively organized within their respective countries and more vigorously supported by their respective governments. The restoration of Europe without a constitution designed to mitigate these rivalries will mean a return to secret diplomacy and the armed peace, preparatory to a reënactment of the great drama which we have just witnessed. What would be left of European civilization after several repetitions of

this cycle may be left to the imagination. But if
Europe cannot learn from experience, it is hardly
probable that more pronunciamentos from Washington will have any effect upon the course of events
there.

Fourthly, there seem to be only two policies open
to the United States. The first is to enter into a
general European council and attempt by international pressure to compel a readjustment of indemnities, debts, tariffs, and currencies; that is, to join
in forcing the various nations to do what they must
do before the course of business is returned to a
pre-war basis. If any one will read the European
press closely, he will see what grave complications
this would involve, what new hatreds, what new
discords. In my opinion it would be unwise for
the United States to attempt to play the part of a
general receiver or a big brother for Europe tor-
tured by the inevitable after-war hatreds. This
is not because we are wanting in the spirit of help-
fulness, but because in this case intermeddling is
likely to do more harm than good. The other
course is that now pursued, except as far as Russia
is concerned. It is the course of allowing Europe
to set its own house in order under the stress of its
own necessities and experiences. Its statesmen
know little enough, perhaps, but they know Europe
better than any agents sent out from Washington.

Fifthly, if the United States leaves Europe to its
own devices in recovering its economic prosperity,
then logic as well as common decency requires our
government to refrain from publishing periodi-

cal homilies on the place of Russia in Europe's affairs.

Sixthly, new loans to European countries by American banking houses, though they yield high commissions and high interest rates at present, merely add to the burdens and confusion of Europe and help postpone the day of fiscal reckoning which all continental countries must face sooner or later. Indeed these very loans may involve us, in spite of ourselves, in grave problems of readjustment now facing European statesmen.

Finally, the menaces that confront the United States today are not European. As President Harding has said, they are in the Pacific. What does that mean? What does it imply in terms of American policy and of obligations for American citizens? President Harding has given us the key. He says that we do not want any more territory in the Pacific, but that we want trade. That means, in plain English, that we want markets in China in which to sell goods; we want opportunities to invest money with good commissions and high rates of interest; and we want concessions to build railways, exploit natural resources, and develop Chinese industries to our profit. Assuming that the open door is really open, that means intense and active rivalry with England, France, and Japan in the Far East. So the great question is: "Shall the government follow trade and investments?"

That is the crucial question. It is a question fraught with momentous significance for this country. Behind all the notes, treaties, speeches, and

declarations, that is the one great issue in foreign
affairs before the people of this country. It must
be considered without bitterness or partisan rancor
in the light of national interests and national destiny. There must be no sneering criticism of our
manufacturers and bankers. They are following
economic opportunities as other men do. Nothing
short of the interest of the whole nation should
come into the decisions upon policy.

At this fateful juncture in American history,
there are three courses open to those who fain
would mould the world to their hearts' desires.
There is first the policy of positive imperialism,
naked and unashamed. Under it, our government
would give vigorous support to merchants, bankers, and manufacturers in all parts of the earth in
their search for trade and investment opportunities.
It presupposes armies and navies adequate to all
exigencies and strong enough to compel respect
for all decisions taken in behalf of national economic interests. The Department of State, operating mainly in secret through a corps of consuls
and diplomats, would become the adjunct to industrial and investment interests. A merchant
marine would be subsidized, and government support given to the prosecution of commercial advantages. Discriminatory and preferential tariffs
would be constructed with reference to the promo-
tion of American industries.

This policy is commonly defended on two grounds.
Some say that it is the natural, inevitable, and irresistible development of an imperial race—the

manifest destiny of every nation to expand, conquer, and dominate. Possibly it is the decree of fate. If so, then all arguments for and against it are equally futile and irrelevant.

Others, brushing aside such philosophy, say that imperialism is necessary to American prosperity, that we must sell more and more manufactured goods every year or perish. Let us examine briefly that hypothesis in operation. More billions in trade means bringing more business to American manufacturing industries and drawing more millions of people from Europe and from our own countryside into mines, mills, and factories. It means more billions in stocks and bonds in strong boxes and more millions of men, women, and children in industrial cities—a vaster aristocracy of wealth and a hugher proletariat. Whoever can contemplate the possibility of a hundred years of that development without thought of consequences lying beyond, deserves to wear the badge of courage. Still the policy involved in it may be pursued without regard to the long future.

Imperialism is not new. It offers no novel features to the adventurous spirit of man. The past affords ample records for the study of its processes, operations, and consequences. It cannot however be pursued today under the conditions of the past three hundred years. The experience of the British Empire is no guide to us now. The backward places of the earth are all staked out and in the possession of powers bent upon the kind of commercial and financial imperialism that is recommended to us. Imperialism of the future will involve competitive risks far more dangerous than the risks of Pitt, Disraeli, and Sir Edward Grey. Still the policy is an intelligible one and is defended by some of the ablest minds of our generation. Ample support for it is to be found in the voluminous literature of the late German empire.

There is before us, possibly, a second policy. It is covered by that term of opprobrium hurled at it by the devotees of imperialism, namely, "Little Americanism." Its implications are likewise clear. Let us examine them. According to this philosophy, the government of the United States would not lend diplomatic or any other kind of support to investment bankers placing loans abroad, either in making them, collecting the interest, or insuring the principal. It would not use the army or the navy in the collection of debts due to private citizens. The government would feel under no greater obligation to a banker who made a bad loan in Guatemala than it would to a banker who made a bad guess in lending money to a dry goods merchant in Des Moines, Iowa. It would not seize any more territory. It would discontinue the policy of annexing spheres in the Caribbean and would invite the Latin-American countries into a coöperative system for settling all disputes in this hemisphere. It would give independence to the Philippines and draw back upon the Hawaiian base. It would maintain an army and a navy adequate for the defense of our territories, by universal service if necessary, and perhaps preferably. It might possibly contemplate entering a League of Nations, provided all other countries were prepared to adopt a similar domestic policy. It would bend all national energies and all national genius upon the creation of a civilization which, in power and glory and noble living, would rise above all the achievements of the past. This policy, whatever may be said against it, has on its side at least the advantage and interest of novelty. The great power that pursued it might, indeed, sink down into dust like the empires of Tamerlane or Augustus, but at least the world's experiences would be enriched.

There is finally another alternative, that of no policy at all, save the policy of drift and muddle. It would support our capitalists and merchants abroad, but not adequately. It would encourage them to pursue their economic interests and then fail to sustain them in a crucial hour. It would create, inadvertently, situations calling for imperial military and naval forces, but would not have the forces ready on the fateful day. It would follow in the paths of Alexander and Caesar but would be content with the philosophy of Buncombe County. Yet, under Providence many things might be accomplished by this policy. It might land the nation at the gates of destruction; but that can be said of the imperial policy pursued by Rome and Germany. As in individual life we find our little plans and purposes but frail reeds in our hands, so in national life, the wisdom, understanding, and penetration of the best and most practical statesmen often prove to be in the test of time and circumstance the weirdest of delusions.

Here I take leave of the subject, saying with Bossuet, the good bishop: "All those who are engaged in the work of government are subject to a higher power. They always do more or less than they intend and their counsels have never failed to produce unforeseen effects. They are not the masters of the turn given to affairs by the ages past. Neither can they foresee the course the future will take. Far less can they force it." Still who would not rather have the heritage of Athens than the legacy of Caesar?

AUTHORITIES

The best account of English diplomacy before the War is Earl Loreburn, *How the War Came* (Knopf, 1920). Sir Edward Grey's speech on August 3, 1914 is printed as an Appendix. For a vigorous indictment of English diplomacy, E. D. Morel, *Ten Years of Secret Diplomacy* and *Truth and the War* (Huebsch, 1912 and 1918); also Francis Neilson, *How Diplomats Make War* and Albert Jay Nock, *The Myth of a Guilty Nation* (Huebsch). A general brief survey, Reinsch, *Secret Diplomacy* (Harcourt, 1922).

The great German collection is *Die Deutschen Dokumente zum Kriegsausbruch* in four volumes (Charlottenburg, 1919). A splendid survey of these materials is given by Professor Sidney B. Fay in the *American Historical Review*, for July and October, 1920. In 1919 the German Government instituted a committee of inquiry which has been investigating the origins of the war. Two volumes have already been printed and a new series of fifteen volumes is announced as in press *(American Historical Review,* October 1921, p. 178).

The Austrian materials are not quite so voluminous. There is first a three volume collection, *Diplomatische Aktenstücke zur Vorgeschichte des Krieges, 1914.* These papers cover the negotiations immediately preceding the war. They have been carefully analyzed by Professor Fay in the articles cited above. A second group of papers is A. F. Pribram, *The Secret Treaties of Austria-Hungary*. These go back to the treaty of alliance of 1879. The first volume embraces treaties and the second collateral documents and notes. They appear in English translation under the editorship of Professor A. C. Coolidge of Harvard University (Harvard Press).

The most important French contribution is the *Livre Jaune de 1918,* which contains materials relative to the Russian Alliance. Selected and published by the French Government. Most of them are reproduced with comment by Welschinger, *L'Alliance Franco-Russe* (Alcan, 1919).

The Russian materials are widely scattered. Apparently there has been no such grand collection as the German Government had prepared. Shortly after they came to power, the Bolsheviki began to publish treaties and notes. The so-called Secret Treaties revealing the agreements among the Entente Allies as to territorial dispositions were published in November, 1917, and shortly afterward appeared in translation in the New York *Evening Post* and the Manchester *Guardian*. A Russian edition in English, with a foreword by Leon Trotzky was also printed about the same time. Copies in the New York Public Library. From time to time additional papers from the Russian archives were published in the official organs *Isvestia* and *Pravda*. Files in the New York Public Library. Some of these papers were translated by the German Government and included in its *Deutschland Schuldig? Deutsches Weissbuch über die Verantwortlichkeit der Urheber des Krieges* (1919).   This appears in English translation also by the Germans: *Is Germany Guilty?   German White Book Concerning the Responsibility of the Authors of the War* (Berlin, Heymanns, 1919).   The chief collection of Russian papers is Siebert and Schreiner, *Entente Diplomacy and the World,* a volume of 762 pages in English translation.   Published privately in New York by the Knickerbocker Press (1921) and for sale by Stechert and also by Brentano.   Baron Siebert, a former secretary of the Imperial Russian Embassy in London, brings out these documents and vouches for their authenticity.   Many of them can be checked up by notes from the German archives and by papers printed in *Pravda* and *Isvestia*.   While it is not possible to verify and authenticate from official evidence all these papers and while it must be remembered that the collections are fragmentary, they do seem to fix beyond all question the broad outlines of European diplomacy between 1908 and 1917.

A new, authentic collection of Russian documents has just come from Paris: *Un Livre Noir: Diplomatie d'Avant-Guerre d'après les Documents des Archives Russes.*   Préface par René Marchand. An admirable review by Baron Korff appears in the *American Historical Review* for July, 1922.

BIBLIOGRAPHY

Alexinsky, G., *La Russie Moderne* and *La Russie et l'Europe.*

Angell, Norman, *The Fruits of Victory.*

Bass and Moulton, *America and the Balance Sheet of Europe* (1921).

Baumont et Berthelot, *L'Allemagne: Lendemains de Guerre et de Révolution* (1922).

Boret, V., *La Bataille Économique de Demain* (1918) Forcasting the economic war after war.

Bouton, S. M., *And the Kaiser Abdicates.*

Brailsford, H. N., *After the Peace.*

Brunet, R., *La Constitution Allemande* (1921) Translation published by Knopf (New York) in 1922.

Conference on the Limitation of Armaments (Washington Conference Documents) Senate Document, 67th Congress, 2nd Session, Number 125, 1922.

Cumming and Pettit, *Russian-American Relations* (1920).

Decrees and Constitution of Soviet Russia (New York Nation Reprint).

Delaisi, F., *Oil: Its influence on Politics.*

Demangeon, *Le Déclin de l'Europe* (1920). To be had in English translation.

Driault, E., *Les Traditions Politiques de la France.*

Dutt, R. P., (ed), *The Labour International Handbook* (1921) Allen and Unwin.

Férasson, L., *La Question du Fer* (1918).

Gautier, *L'Angleterre et Nous* (1922).

Graham, S., *Europe—Whither Bound?* (1922).

Grumbach, S., *Das Annexionistische Deutschland* (1917).

Guest, L. H,. *The Struggle for Power in Europe, 1917-1921* (1922).

Jouhaux, L., *Le Syndicalisme et la C. G. T.* (1920).

Keynes, J. M., *The Economic Consequences of the Peace* and *A Revision of the Treaty.*

Lanessan, *Histoire de l'Entente Cordiale Franco-Anglaise* (1916).

Leger, L., *Le Panslavisme et l'Intérêt Français.*

Lenin, N., *The Proletariat Revolution; The Soviets at Work; The Land Revolution in Russia;* and *Les Bolcheviks et les Paysans.*

Lichtenberger et Petit, *L'Impérialisme Économique Allemand.*

Marx, H., *Handbuch der Revolution in Deutschland* (1919).

Morel, *Africa and the Peace of Europe.*

Pasvolsky, L., *The Economics of Communism* and *Russia and the Far East.*

Pratt, E. A., *Rise of Rail-Power in War and Conquest.*

Scheidemann, P., *Der Zusammenbruch* (1921).

"Spectator," *Das Socialisierungsproblem in Deutschland* (1920).

Spengler, O., *Preussentum und Sozialismus* (1921).

Stier-Somlo, *Reichsverfassung* (1919).

Streit, C., *Where Iron is, There is the Fatherland.*

Tarlé, A., *La Préparation de la Lutte Éconimique par l'Allemagne* (1919).

Trotzky, L., *From October to Brest Litovsk; Terrorisme et Communisme;* and *Les Soviets et l'Imperialisme Mondial.*

Vanderlip, F. A., *What Next in Europe?*

Wells, H. G., *Washington and the Riddle of Peace.*

THE END